accountability for the South African public service, bringing to light an aspect of ethics and accountable governance in Africa's public sector from South Africa in the aftermath of 'State Capture', which had eroded public service probity.

## Part II: Governance and Public Sector Performance

Chapter 6 (Metz), 'An African Moral Theory and Public Governance: Nepotism, Preferential Hiring, and Other Partiality' is the first chapter in Part II: 'Governance and Public Sector Performance'. It argues in favour of a 'moderate partialism', a normative political philosophy which may allow a government agent to rightly favour at some cost to the public veterans and victims of state injustices, but not those in their family or party. The chapter seeks to provide a new, unified explanation of why characteristically sub-Saharan African values permit some forms of partiality, such as the preferential hiring of those who suffered from or struggled against colonialism, but forbid other, nepotistic or prebendalist, forms of partiality.

Part II: 'Governance and Public Sector Performance' continues in Chap. 7 (Wenyah), 'Africa's Public Sector and Anti-Corruption Initiatives—A Focus on Ghana'. This chapter seeks to understand how a wide spectrum of anti-corruption initiatives (national, regional, continental and global) in all regions of the African continent have been able to tackle corruption. With a concentration on Ghana, the chapter provides some recommendations that could help improve the attainment of the goals of the anti-corruption initiatives.

Nwokolo continues the interesting journey in Part II by working on Chap. 8 'Public Service Performance Management'. The chapter explores the impact of two dimensions of management practice in public service delivery: autonomy provided to bureaucrats; and provision of incentives to and monitoring of bureaucrats. By examining the management practices of bureaucrats in African countries such as Nigeria, Ghana and Uganda, the chapter provides the score cards of these dimensions on public service performance.

Chapter 9 (Ayentimi), 'Leveraging Public Service Performance Management to Enhance Public Service Delivery—A Contemporary Perspective' is the penultimate chapter of Part II section of the book. The author opines that leveraging public service performance management to enhance public service delivery remains a global priority as public service organisations across the globe are under increasing pressure to deliver quality public service. The chapter further highlights the landscape of public service performance management in Africa, with a focus on the underlying complications undermining its effectiveness and success. In conclusion, the chapter explores how Africa can leverage performance management to enhance the efficiency of public service.

The final chapter of Part II (and the book) is Chap. 10 (Ogunyemi, Adisa and Hinson), 'Accountable Governance and Ethical Practice in Africa's Public Sector—Mapping a Path for the Future'. The chapter unequivocally claims that gaps in good governance and ethical conduct impede growth and development in Africa. On the basis of the submissions by the chapters' authors in the book, this chapter advocates for good leadership and ethical renaissance in public office holders as a condition precedent to stem the trend of unethical and unacceptable behaviour in African public institutions. As a final note, the editors affirm that through the findings and recommendations of authors in this book, there is a path for the future of accountable governance in Africa.

Faculty, Lagos Business School                    Professor Akintola Owolabi
Pan-Atlantic University, Nigeria

# Contents

# Notes on Contributors

**Isaiah Adisa** is a management researcher and consultant based in Nigeria. He holds an MSc degree in Industrial Relations and Human Resource Management from the Olabisi Onabanjo University, Ago-Iwoye, Nigeria. He has co-edited book(s) on green marketing and green people management. He has co-authored book chapters and journal articles to his name. His research interests cut across human resources management, organisational behaviour, marketing, and gender studies.

**Desmond Tutu Ayentimi** is Associate Fellow Higher Education Academy and Senior Lecturer in Management in the Tasmanian School of Business and Economics, University of Tasmania, Hobart. He holds a PhD in Management from Curtin University, Western Australia. His research interests include multinational enterprises HRM, technology and employment relations, cross-cultural management, diversity, equality and inclusion and HRD in sub-Saharan Africa. His articles have been published extensively in reputable international journals including *Industrial Relations Journal, Personnel Review, Education + Training, Asia Pacific Journal of Human Resources, Thunderbird International Business Review, Technology Analysis and Strategic Management* and *Journal of Social Entrepreneurship.*

**Isaac Sewornu Coffie** is a final year PhD candidate at the University of Ghana Business School. He obtained his master's degree in Marketing at the Department of Marketing and Entrepreneurship of the same university. His teaching and research areas include social marketing, corporate social responsibility, entrepreneurship and market orientation. He has over 12 years of corporate working experience as a marketing executive and is an entrepreneur.

**Emmanuel Etim** is a doctoral student with the Department of Public Administration, Lagos State University, and a researcher at Lagos Business School, Pan-Atlantic University. He holds a Bachelor of Science degree and a master's degree in Public Administration and Political Science, respectively. He also has an Advanced Diploma in Business Management and Leadership. Before joining Lagos Business School, Etim lectured at the Lagos State Polytechnic, where he taught business research methods. He has also worked in the Office of the Permanent Secretaries, Lagos State Ministry of Special Duties and Intergovernmental Relations and Lagos State Ministry of Education, in Alausa, Lagos State. He is a Certified Asian Reviewer and has co-authored more than twenty articles in reputable international and local journals and some book chapters. He has attended and presented papers at many conferences and has won many awards.

**Robert E. Hinson** is the Deputy Vice Chancellor (Academic) at the University of Kigali. He is also Visiting Professor of Marketing at the Lincoln International Business School, Professor of Marketing at the University of Ghana, and Extraordinary Professor of Marketing at the University of the Free State Business School. He holds a DPhil in Marketing from the University of Ghana and a PhD in International Business from the Aalborg University Business School.

**Nkemdilim Iheanachor** is a member of the Strategy Group in Lagos Business School (LBS). Iheanachor holds a bachelor's degree in Electronic Engineering, an MBA, as well as MPhil and PhD degrees in Management. He is also a visiting lecturer on the MBA programme at the University of Stellenbosch's Business School, Cape Town, South Africa. He is a member of the Academy of Management, Academy of International Business and the Academy of Innovation, Entrepreneurship & Knowledge. He is a member of the editorial boards of the *International Journal of Governance* *and Financial Intermediation* and *ESIC Digital Economy and Innovation Journal.*

**Thaddeus Metz** is Professor of Philosophy at the University of Pretoria. He is known for drawing on the African philosophical tradition analytically to address a variety of contemporary moral/political/legal controversies. Metz has had more than 300 books, chapters, and articles published, including *A Relational Moral Theory: African Ethics in and Beyond the Continent* (2021). His next book addressing African philosophy, to be titled *A Relational Theory of Justice*, is under contract (with Oxford University Press).

**Khali Mofuoa** is a research associate in the Department of Philosophy, University of Pretoria. He has a PhD in Professional and Applied Ethics from Charles Sturt University in Australia. He is an experienced ethics practitioner and a GRC professional with great passion for ethics. He previously worked for Vodacom Group and, most recently, Road Accident Fund as the head of Ethics Office responsible for ethics management. He is a seasoned corporate ethics training facilitator with more than 15 years. He is a certified ethics officer and an associate of the Ethics Institute. He is a member of South African Institute of Chartered Accountants (SAICA) Ethics Committee. His life motto is "Cur non ego—why not I".

**Mpfareleni Mavis Netswera** is a post-doctoral fellow in the Department of Public Administration and Management at the University of South Africa. Prior, she was a postgraduate fellow and lecturer in the same department whilst pursuing her PhD. She has more than a decade as a social researcher in the public service. She has published on local government elections and community participation. Her research interests are public policy, intergovernmental relations, service delivery, ethics and public participation.

**Fulufhelo Netswera** is a social science research professor and an executive dean of the Faculty of Management Sciences at the Durban University of Technology. He writes in public accountability and service delivery.

**Arinze Nwokolo** is a lecturer in the Department of Accounting, Economics and Finance at Lagos Business School (LBS), Pan-Atlantic University. He graduated from the University of Navarra with a PhD in

Economics and Business Administration in 2017. His research comprises public policy topics in developing countries, including the impact of positive oil price shocks on the monopoly of violence and consolidation of power by governments in Nigeria; the long-term effect of the free health care at birth on adult mental health in South Africa; and the impact of terrorism on local trust and ethnic identification in Nigeria. Prior to joining Lagos Business School, Nwokolo was a CSAE fellow in Oxford University and a research associate at the Navarra International Development Centre, Spain.

**Kemi Ogunyemi** holds a degree in Law from the University of Ibadan, an LLM from the University of Strathclyde, and MBA and PhD degrees from Pan-Atlantic University. She teaches business ethics, managerial anthropology, self-leadership and sustainability management at the Lagos Business School. She is also the director of the Christopher Kolade Centre for Research in Leadership and Ethics as well as the academic director for the School's Senior Management Programme. Her consulting and research interests include personal ethos, work-life ethic, social responsibility, sustainability, governance, and anti-corruption action. She has authored and edited numerous publications including *Responsible Management: Understanding Human Nature, Ethics, and Sustainability, Teaching Ethics across the Management Curriculum,* and *African Virtue Ethics Traditions for Business and Management.*

**Samuel Wenyah** is a political researcher and a climate scientist. He works as the programme coordinator of the University of Ghana Plastic Recycling Project (UGPRP), the first public university recycling initiative of its kind in the West African sub-region. He possesses a bachelor's degree in Political Science and a master's degree in Climate Change and Sustainable Development. Aside his profound interests in climate change, Wenyah has keen interests in issues of ethics and accountable governance in African politics. As a researcher, he is well abreast with the existing political landscape on the African continent and has been involved in numerous research projects in this area.

# List of Figures

# List of Tables

# Part I

Ethics and Ethical Compliance

2006; Purwanto, Mukharrom, Zhilyakov, Pamuji, & Shankar, 2019; Sroka & Lőrinczy, 2015; Trevino & Nelson, 2016).

In addition to academic scholars, business practitioners' interests in ethical leadership (Heyler et al., 2016) also appear to have increased and become central in driving a global focus on the need for a higher moral standard and consistently ethical behaviour on the part of corporate managers and business organisations (Bazerman & Sezer, 2016; Karassavidou & Glaveli, 2006). The widely publicised ethical misconducts involving WorldCom, Arthur Andersen, Tyco and Enron, among others, highlighted the importance of the issue for the private sector (Bazerman & Sezer, 2016) and emphasised that gaps in ethical conduct occur across both developed and developing economies, and in both private and public sectors (Albaum & Peterson, 2006).

Turning back to the public sector in Africa, the focus of this book, we now consider the argument of Hope (1999) that governance gaps in Africa reflect a climate of unethical leadership throughout most of the continent. Two years after his work, in 2001, the UNDP published a two-volume report titled 'Public Service Ethics in Africa'[1] in which they found, amongst other things, that:

- African countries have values, standards, and laws against corruption, unethical acts, and incidents of maladministration. However, the laws are sometimes outdated and may not sufficiently cover technical developments or social trends.
- There are difficulties in applying existing specific anti-corruption laws due to the complexity of the text and the onerous burden of proof in a crime that is often not visible.
- The management and control of the conduct of public servants continue to be problematic.
- Whilst many anti-corruption institutions have been moderately effective in fighting corruption and unethical behaviour, the lack of sufficient resources to adequately fulfil their mandate remains a major problem.

---

[1] https://publicadministration.un.org/publications/content/PDFs/E-Library%20Archives/2001%20Public%20Service%20Ethics%20in%20Africa,%20Vol.%201.pdf

- The prevention of outright corruption or even of inadvertent violation of standards through ethics education, advice and or counselling has not been given proper attention.
- Governments need to enhance their transparency by sharing information about their activities.

The findings above pointed to great opportunities to improve public service ethics in Africa yet the situation two decades later does not seem very different. Africa currently faces enormous challenges in its efforts to achieve sustainable human development. The public service, as an institution, has a critical role to play in the development of a nation. When the public service is weak and underperforming, the private sector might also not experience the resilience it deserves. These phenomena are not unique to Africa. Poor ethical culture is a menace to achieving public sector efficiency and thus to sustainable development anywhere in the world. This is why this new book on accountable governance and ethical conduct in Africa is timely as it explores the challenges faced in the continent in the public sector ethics, uncovers the underlying reasons, and offers possible solutions that could be hinged on leveraging healthier political systems, greater inclusivity, and /or more extensive digitalisation.

Accountability is the cornerstone of good governance, says Adejuwon (2012), and it involves answerability and enforcement (Adejuwon 2012). If, as stated above, accountability and good governance have been a problem due to lack of implementation and proper monitoring of public sector codes of ethics and behaviour, leaders in the sector need to implement the codes and lead by example, demonstrating the expected behaviour and beginning a new wave of ethical public service institution. Adejuwon (2012) suggests that when government leaders explain and justify their decision to the agencies and committees that necessarily serve as checks and balances, the display of transparency and accountability is bound to have a ripple effect in the rest of the public sector by inspiring their followers to act similarly.

Accountability and answerability place expectations on the government agencies to explain the why, what and how of their actions to the general public. In addition, the agencies in charge of monitoring and evaluation of government services must be given the power to sanction fore the challenges that the individual public official faces in situations of conflict of interest, when personal interest is pitted against the public interest he or she is sworn to promote and protect. They discuss at length and make recommendations for guidance.

Coming on their heels, Netswera (Chap. 4) exposes the results of badly managed conflicts of interest during the COVID 19 pandemic in South Africa. Now the reader has a specific country case study that illustrates the importance of public actors being sincere in their committing to serve and taking pride in being accountable despite a strong temptation to enrich themselves. One could even argue that, for a person that has entered public service, the burden of responsibility to practice ethics (honesty, fairness, inclusion, etc.) is higher than that of private sector actors because the person has stepped forward to present himself or herself as a worthy steward of public resources and the public good. The person has accepted (and in many cases, actively sought) a fiduciary position which only truly selfless people deserve to occupy. In the face of the tough choices that the public official is facing, the principle of *Thuma Mina* provides refreshment and relief (Mofuoa, Chap. 5).

Mofuoa in Chap. 5 provides for us an African variant of the third main ethical theory, virtue theory, which is older indeed than the two already presented by Iheanachor and Etim, and completive to them. Where rules and consequences fall short in prescribing ethical behaviour, moral character which is central to the virtue ethics theory is in place to empower the public official to do the right thing. Sometimes there are no rules, or the rules are not enforced, or the rules are inadequate; sometimes the consequences are not easily evaluable since some are intangible and appearances can be deceptive; however, the ethical person does not depend only on external motivations (rules, consequences) to make ethical choices. The ethical person develops an internal moral compass through gradual growth in wisdom and in self-discipline that comes from the practice of virtue. Thus it is with the public official who acknowledges that he or she is 'sent' and thus finds intrinsic reasons to withstand corruption even, at times, at great personal cost.

Having achieved some understanding of the ethical issues facing the public official and the ways to confront them in part 1, we move on to part 2 where the level of analysis is the larger community. Here the first major contribution is from Metz, who lays the foundation for systemic change in the African narrative by highlighting an African value system in such a way as to distinguish the fine line between nepotism and communitarianism. This line of African philosophical thought presented by Metz (Chap. 6) constitutes one way to navigate the rough seas of a species of conflict-of-interest situations. According to him, as a people, we know the difference and we can do the right thing without using one situation to rationalise or to cover up the other. In Metz's contribution, we have a systemic value-based approach to resolving Africa's governance problems. However, what can one approach to one issue achieve given the multiplicity of cultures and challenges facing the different African countries? Wenyah (Chap. 7) brings to light the rule-oriented and complementary systemic approaches to sanitising the climate in which individuals act so that they find support to do what is right—by exploring the vast arena of anti-corruption initiatives in Africa. In doing this, Wenyah provides some hope that things are working albeit slowly.

The chapters following Wenyah go further to turn the spotlight from anti-corruption onto the management of performance in Africa's public sector and the ways to leverage it for improved service delivery. These next two authors also take up the conversation at a systemic rather than individual level and show how public service delivery must be effective for the economy to grow and for the rich-poor divide to become narrower (Arinze, Chap. 8) and for the public service to truly serve the people it was set up to serve (Ayentimi, Chap. 9). Thus, one looks to the impact of performance management on the continent's development while the other looks at its impact on the service rendered by the public sector. Ayentimi explains the concept of performance management and its role in supporting the achievement of the organisation's strategic goals. It would seem that the public service goals cannot be achieved if performance management is not well-designed and well-executed—Ayentimi uses the experience of the operational difficulties in responding to the. Covid-19 pandemic is a case in point to emphasise where performance could be managed better so as to ensure service delivery. In full agreement that performance management would make public service bureaucracies work more efficiently Arinze (Chap. 8) suggests that bureaucrats should have greater autonomy, well-structured incentives, and adequate monitoring. Finally, in the last chapter of the book, we again state the need for accountable leadership and governance for the public sector in Africa and, using the content of the preceding chapters, suggest the path to the future.

## Conclusion

The need for better governance in Africa is urgent. It is one important way to make developmental goals and plans realisable. Making the change from the current reality requires African leaders to lead by example by initiating and abiding by ethical values that will promote the right public service behaviour. Modelling from leaders in every level—small teams, larger teams, agencies and parastatals, the local governments, states, and the countries, will make a big difference to Africa's levels of accountable governance.

This is not enough, however. People management policies and practices in the public sector must also improve. For example, the challenge of unfair pay is real: when governments do not see and act on the need to take care of the welfare of public servants with reasonable remuneration and basic benefits, the environment creates pressure to engage in unethical practices in order to supplement earnings. Without excusing their bad actions, one can understand that when public servants are not well remunerated at work, they may easily rationalise unethical behaviour and justify what they do by pointing to unjust pay or to the unethical models they have around them.

In addition, the implementation and monitoring of policies geared towards ensuring accountability are crucial and need to be supported strongly. So long as policies and laws are not adequately implemented and monitored, people may use that as an excuse to give in to corruption. With courageous and consistent value-based and purpose-driven strategic actions, such as returning to indigenous wisdom principles such as *Thuma Mina* (the sent leader) and putting systems in place to achieve anti-corruption compliance and to foster equitable and efficient service delivery through performance management, the future could be really promising for Africa.

# References

Adejuwon, K. D. (2012). The dilemma of accountability and good governance for improved public service delivery in Nigeria. *Africa's Public Service Delivery & Performance Review, 1*(3), 25–45.

Adeola, O. (2022). Leveraging trust to enhance the public sector brand in Africa. In R. E. Hinson, N. Madichie, O. Adeola, B. J. Nyigmah, I. Adisa, & K. Asamoah (Eds.), *New public management in Africa. Palgrave studies of public sector management in Africa.* Palgrave Macmillan. https://doi.org/10.1007/978-3-030-77181-2_3

Albaum, G., & Peterson, R. A. (2006). Ethical attitudes of future business leaders: Do they vary by gender and religiosity? *Business & Society, 45*(3), 300–321.

Bazerman, M. H., & Sezer, O. (2016). Bounded awareness: Implications for ethical decision making. *Organisational Behavior and Human Decision Processes, 136*, 95–105.

Casimir, K. C., Izueke, E. M., & Nzekwe, I. F. (2014). Public sector and corruption in Nigeria: An ethical and institutional framework of analysis. *Open Journal of Philosophy, 4*, 216–224.

Cheteni, P., & Shindika, E. S. (2017). Ethical leadership in South Africa and Botswana. *BAR-Brazilian Administration Review, 14*(2), e160077.

Chigudu, D. C. (2018). Corporate governance in Africa's public sector for sustainable development: The task ahead. *TD: The Journal for Transdisciplinary Research in Southern Africa, 14*(1), 1–10.

ElGammal, W., El-Kassar, A.-N., & Canaan Messarra, L. (2018). Corporate ethics, governance and social responsibility in MENA countries. *Management Decision, 56*(1), 273–291.

Fisher, J. (2004). Social responsibility and ethics: Clarifying the concepts. *Journal of Business Ethics, 52*(4), 391–400. https://doi.org/10.2307/25123269

Gichure, C. P. (2015). *Towards instilling ethics in African business and public service: The case of Kenya.* Dspace.

Heyler, S. G., Armenakis, A. A., Walker, A. G., & Collier, D. Y. (2016). A qualitative study investigating the ethical decision making process: A proposed model. *The Leadership Quarterly, 27*(5), 788–801.

Hinson, R. E., Madichie, N., Adeola, O., Nyigmah, B. J., Adisa, I., & Asamoah, K. (2022). New public management in Africa: An introduction. In R. E. Hinson, N. Madichie, O. Adeola, B. J. Nyigmah, I. Adisa, & K. Asamoah (Eds.), *New public management in Africa. Palgrave studies of public sector management in Africa.* Palgrave Macmillan. https://doi.org/10.1007/978-3-030-77181-2_1

Hope, K. R. (1999). *Corruption in Africa: A crisis in ethical leadership.* Westview Press.

Karassavidou, E., & Glaveli, N. (2006). Towards the ethical or the unethical side? An explorative research of Greek business students' attitudes. *International Journal of Educational Management, 20*(5), 348–364. https://doi.org/10.1108/09513540610676421

Nkyabonaki, J. (2019). Effectiveness of the public service code of ethics in controlling corrupt behaviour in the public service: Opinion from the Grassroots at Toangoma Ward-Temeke Municipal Council. *Journal of Asian and African Studies, 54*(8), 1195–1212.

Onyebuchi, V. N. (2011). Ethics in accounting. *International Journal of Business and Social Science, 2*(10), 275–276.

Purwanto, R. M., Mukharrom, T., Zhilyakov, D. I., Pamuji, E., & Shankar, K. (2019). Study the importance of business ethics and ethical marketing in digital era. *Journal of Critical Reviews, 6*(5), 150–154.

Putu, S. N., Jan van Helden, G., & Tillema, S. (2007). Public sector performance measurement in developing countries: A literature review and research agenda. *Journal of Accounting & Organizational Change, 3*(3), 192–208. https://doi.org/10.1108/18325910710820265

Rossouw, G. J. (2005). Business ethics and corporate governance in Africa. *Business & Society, 44*(1), 94–106.

Solomon, R. C. (1994). Business and the humanities: An Aristotelian approach to business ethics. *The Ruffin Series in Business Ethics,* 45–75.

Sroka, W., & Lőrinczy, M. (2015). The perception of ethics in business: Analysis of research results. *Procedia Economics and Finance, 34,* 156–163.

Trevino, L. K., & Nelson, K. A. (2016). *Managing business ethics: Straight talk about how to do it right.* John Wiley & Sons.

# 2

# Ethical Dilemmas and the Changing Reality in Africa's Public Sector

Nkemdilim Iheanachor and Emmanuel Etim

## Introduction

The need to have a clear-cut understanding of what makes up living a worthy life, and the activities required to achieve this goal, remains the core definition of ethics. Ethics is a *philosophy of morality* concerned with the 'ought' and 'ought not' (Mahony, 2009; Ehrich et al., 2011). Notably, this applies in private lives and within the business and corporate environments. Today, experts, researchers, and administration practitioners are interested in ethical leadership, which appears on the front burner of global best practices and improved moral standards in public service. It is instructive to note that African countries have values and laws against misconduct and corrupt practices (Ndeunyema, 2019). Still, these canons are mostly outdated or without sufficient technical developments and substance to address contemporary social trends and demands.

N. Iheanachor (✉) • E. Etim
Lagos Business School, Pan-Atlantic University, Lagos, Nigeria
e-mail: niheanachor@lbs.edu.ng

© The Author(s), under exclusive license to Springer Nature Switzerland AG 2022
K. Ogunyemi et al. (Eds.), *Ethics and Accountable Governance in Africa's Public Sector,
Volume I*, Palgrave Studies of Public Sector Management in Africa,
https://doi.org/10.1007/978-3-030-95394-2_2

Both developed and developing economies are undergoing dramatic changes in the twenty-first century because of the pluralisation of service provisions, and non-linear and wicked problems. Unfortunately, these dramatic changes in contemporary public administration meet a static paradigm to public sector reform and implementation approach in Africa (Ugyel, 2016; Karataş, 2019). From the inception of African public administration to date, various forces—legal, political, social, economic, and technological–have shaped the evolution of ethics, injected opportunities and challenges, and dictated values and dilemmas in every era.

We define ethical dilemmas in this chapter as experiences accompanied by challenging emotions and several options of actions to choose from, resulting in a positive or negative outcome (Okkonen & Takala, 2019). An ethical dilemma occurs when organisational principles and standards conflict with each other during decision-making (Pandiani et al., 1998; Muitaba et al., 2011). Here, a public servant faces two conflicting moral requirements where none overrides the other. This situation is problematic, especially as the African public administration keeps less elastic finalities, structures, contents, forms, and working methods to adapt to the new realities. The changes in modern trends have triggered a departure from 'simple answers' to 'hard questions' (Peters, 2003; Peters & Pierre, 2015). Extant literature has shown the relevance of ethics in public administration and the manner in which civil servants can conduct themselves to gain public trust (Radhika, 2012; Frederickson & Rohr, 2015). However, minor efforts are made to explain what makes up the crux of ethics and the changing realities that bedevil the African public administration. This chapter will take stock of current theoretical and practical developments shaping ethics in modern African public administration. It pays attention to factors such as Covid-19, complexity and wicked problems in the African public sector and seeks to answer the following questions: what values should public servants possess to perform their duties perfectly? What moral standards should inform civil servants' decisions?

teleological ethics, and both are applied in the description of how public officers get into an ethical dilemma and strategies to avoid them. This methodological approach typifies the qualitative mode of inquiry, which the chapter typically exemplifies.

# Overview of the African Public Sector

The wave of increasing debate on the importance of the state in the developmental processes in the 1990s led to the demand fora capable public sector. We cannot over emphasise the relevance of the public sector to the socio-economic development of Africa. According to the World Development Report, "an effective public sector is vital for the provision of the goods and services and the rule and institutions—that allow markets to flourish and the people to lead healthier and happier lives" (World Bank, 1997, p. 1). This implies that sustainable development is impossible without an excellent public sector. We expect public sectors in Africa to meet the public interest by providing essential goods and services made possible by unique and top-quality employees. Unfortunately, the African public sector could not deliver on this expectation through effective service delivery. We have attributed this problem to its accumulation of excessive power, corruption, inconsistent policies, lack of accountability and indifference towards public needs and demands (Ayee, 2012). Today, we have redefined the role of the African public sector because of factors such as ineffectiveness, economic crisis, et cetera. It calls for state-owned organisations to be managed like the private sector to curtail acute cases of ineffectiveness caused by policy inconsistencies. Citizens demand that the African public service comprises willing employees and complies with best practices and ethical standards. The ethical and moral standards of public servants speak volumes to performing such an organisation. Aside from ethical and moral issues, PESTEL (i.e. political, economic, social, technological, environmental, and legal) problems also shape the performance of the public sector, just as it does the private sector.

# Factors That Are Changing the Reality of the African Public Sector

a. *Covid-19*

The outbreak of Covid-19 further complicated the challenges faced by public servants in keeping the medical system functioning, protecting the society and securing business, and keeping the family safe. Today, there is a need for public servants to find novel ways to design strategies to stimulate the economy and manage the severe spikes in unemployment on the continent. Covid-19 has brought about some transformations in work and workplaces in the public sector. Some public servants are now working from home. In the words of Ansell et al. (2020):

> Covid-19 crises have clarified that turbulent problems characterised by dramatic and unpredictable events- persistently disrupt our society and challenge the public sector. The public sector is being tested to its limits by the Covid-19 pandemic, which has swept away the standard repertoire of foresight, protection and resilience strategies and brought society and economy to a slowdown.

From Ansell et al.'s point of view, it's a beacon on the public sector to devise strategies to respond adequately to the challenges posed by the pandemic. Therefore, this demands more attention to be paid to the ethical issue surrounding the discharge of public service in the post-covid-19 era, with careful attention to the moral issue in the public sector that are strong enough to reduce the challenge posed by wicked problems.

b. *Wicked problems*: A wicked problem is a social or cultural problem that defies every attempt to solve. For a problem to be termed 'wicked', it must be complex and inter-connected. Therefore, it is challenging to clarify the aims or the solution to a wicked problem (Head & Alford, 2015). Aside from being subject to real-world constraints, wicked problems hinder risk-free attempts to solve them. Typical examples of wicked problems are poverty, climate change, sustainability, education, and homelessness. For instance, to solve poverty, the seen in the setting and the space that an individual partakes. This implies that dilemmas are ever present in individuals' lives, and a dilemmatic space largely influences public servants' work and lives. This ethical dilemma impacts public servants' relationship with the public.

Many public servants, especially new entrants, experience emotional challenges and often, they see these ethical dilemmas as having no inherent solution. We have also noticed two influential agents of ethical dilemmas in the public sector; the client and the co-workers. As regards the client, the dilemma involves encountering aggressive clients and clients living in poor circumstances. In terms of co-workers, the dilemmatic experience draws mostly from disillusioned and derogatory talks in the office. Usually, new entrants are interested in providing quality service to clients with much care and attention, in contrast to the option for action (Lindqvist et al., 2020) (Fig. 2.2).

It is usually an emotional situation in the public sector, especially for new entrants, when approached by clients living in deplorable conditions. It gets worse when new entrants realise that the poor client visited the wrong office and did not have the means of transporting himself to the actual ministry, department, or agency (MDA) saddled with the responsibility to handle the client's request. Another situation is printing, photocopying and typing necessary documents or paying for passport size photograph to be used to process the poor client's request. Many public servants have been in this dilemma space at least once or many times in their careers.

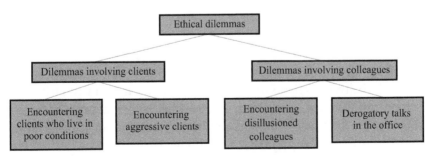

**Fig. 2.2** Ethical dilemmas. (Source: Authors' compilation [2021])

## Encountering Aggressive Clients

Public servants in Africa experience aggression from clients. This is done to fellow clients, a colleague, or themselves. It is often dilemmatic when the organisation seems incapable of handling these aggressions. Here, public servants are restrained by extant laws, rules and regulations and cannot act in a way they considered morally right, even when a couple of them would have loved to use their moral compass in such situations (Davies & Heyward, 2019). New entrants into the public service are often frustrated in the face of this situation. They feel they could better have applied their physical strength or ingenuity in handling the problem, but for existing administrative laws and principles.

## Encountering Disillusioned Colleagues

The African public service is full of rational ambiguity. This subjects many employees to a reasonable space they thought of as being negative. The existence of laws and regulations in the public service does not wipe away the fact that people are still entitled to their opinions on what they feel is rational. However, in situations like this, it is often important to align with what the rule says. This alignment speaks to the uniformity that is expected in service delivery and helps to build clients' trust. When the laws and regulations are strictly adhered to, all clients are going to enjoy equal treatments, except where there are exemptions that are well-known. It is instructive to note that whether uniformity exists, the buzz-word to remember is 'client's satisfaction'. Here, new entrants and junior staff often feel they want to help and pay more attention to satisfy all client requests, but have limited option of carrying out the tasks, especially when they work under a disillusioned supervisor. Disillusioned public servants are hostile towards their profession. Here, amidst several jobs to be delivered, clients to be attended to in minimal time, the incompetent (disillusioned) staffs seem less worried. New entrants and junior teams under the supervision of these civil servants end up learning either nothing or a negative approach to staff-client relationships in the public sector.

Peters, B. G. (2003). The changing nature of public administration: From easy answers to hard questions. *Public Policy and Administration, 1*(5), 7–20.

Peters, B. G., & Pierre, J. (2015). Governance and civil service systems: From easy answers to hard questions. In *Comparative civil service systems in the 21st century* (pp. 286–300). Palgrave Macmillan.

Puiu, S. (2015). Ethics management in public sector—Background and tools. *Procedia Economics and Finance, 23*, 604–607.

Radhika, D. (2012). Ethics in public administration. *Journal of Public Administration and Policy Research, 4*(2), 23–31.

Shapira-Lishchinsky, O. (2010). Ethical dilemmas in teaching and nursing: The Israeli case. *Oxford Review of Education, 36*(6), 731–748.

Traer, R. (2013). Ethics and science: Moral consideration. In *Doing environmental ethics* (2nd ed., pp. 21–39). Westview Press.

Ugyel, L. (2016). *Paradigms and public sector reform: Public administration of Bhutan*. Palgrave Macmillan.

Weber, J. (2008). Dilemmas, ethical. In R. W. Kolb (Ed.), *Encyclopedia of business ethics and society* (pp. 592–593). Sage.

World Bank. (1997). *World Development Report, 1997: The state in a changing world*. The World Bank.

Yung, B. (2016). Introduction: Ethical dilemmas, social values and public policy: The context of governance and citizenship. In B. Yung & K.-P. Yu (Eds.), *Ethical dilemmas in public policy: The dynamics of social values in the East-west context of Hong Kong* (pp. 1–20). Springer.

is required. This often entails public officials being required to disclose potential conflicts of interest as well as the establishment of a conflict of interest management rules and procedures (Munzhedzi, 2016; Ochoa & Graycar, 2016; OECD, 2006). For instance, Munzhedzi's (2016) work indicates that civil society organisations and other key stakeholders are convinced that, to reduce the danger of corruption in Sub-Saharan Africa, conflict of interest must be identified, managed, and, if possible, avoided. Thus, building trust is a severe integrity factor for governmental agencies and individual civil officials.

A conflict of interest may be actual or potential (Vanagas & Juškys, 2019). It is actual when the official's private interest is already in conflict with their official duty to act in the public interest. A possible conflict of interest occurs when an official's private-capacity interest does not yet conflict with their responsibility to act in the public interest, but it may in the future. The likelihood that a possible conflict of interest will become an actual conflict of interest is determined by the public official's duties and the private interest at hand.

# Conflicts of Interest and Corruption

According to Catchick (2014), conflict of interest is an integral ingredient of corruption, and that corruption cannot exist without conflict of interest. Thus, almost all corruption cases involve a conflict of interest, but the reverse might not be true. For instance, Wu and Sun (2014) argue that identifying and effectively managing or preventing a conflict of interest is an effective means of fighting corruption at the early stage. Spence (2004) also concluded that one of the most important enablers of corruption in most public sector organisations is the conflict of interest. Ayee (2008) further theorised that the fundamental factor driving most corrupt practices on the African continent is a conflict of interest and that addressing conflict of interest will significantly minimise the incidence of corruption in the sub-region. For instance, the findings of Osei-Tutu et al. (2014) show a positive correlation between conflict of interest and corrupt practices in the Ghanaian construction sector. The findings of Munzhedzi (2016) also suggest that the main reason for the rife corruption in the South African public sector is conflict of interest and non-adherence to public policy. These empirical findings support the argument that minimising conflict of interest is most likely to reduce the incidence of corruption, particularly in public sector institutions in Africa, and for that matter, Ghana. In other words, the importance of addressing conflicts of interest (COI) in the fight against corruption is becoming increasingly necessary in the fight against corruption.

# Efforts by the Ghanaian Government to Address the Menace of Conflict of Interest

The Ghanaian governments have made several efforts to manage and address the issue of conflict of interest through legislation and enforcement (Rahman, 2018). By way of commitment to the fight against conflict of interest and its related corrupt practices, the supreme law of the country—the Constitution, clearly stipulates means by which to effectively manage or deal with situations of conflict of interest whenever they arise. For example, Article 284 of the 1992 Constitution states, "a public officer shall not put himself in a situation where his personal interests conflict or are likely to conflict with the discharge of the tasks of his office."

The Commission on Human Rights and Administrative Justice (CHRAJ) was established in October 1993, following Ghana's return to constitutional, civilian democratic rule in 1992. It brought together three organisations under one roof: a human rights institution, an ombudsman, and an Anti-Corruption Agency. One of the objectives for establishing the Commission was to address conflict of interest situations by investigating allegations of public officials who had violated or failed to follow Article 284 of the Constitution. This article states that a public officer shall not place himself in a situation where his personal interests conflict with or are likely to conflict with the fulfilment of the officer's functions (CHRAJ, 2005). The Commission also has the mandate to promote the integrity of public institutions through education (Odoi, 2021; CHRAJ, 2005). The Constitution guarantees its independence, requirements. It also observed that the "Respondent is either a director, former director or shareholder, or beneficial owner, of several companies whose objects relate to the securities market sector." The companies include Databank and EGL. As such, the Respondent's interests in the growth and well-being of those companies can conflict with the state's interests in relation to the securities market, such as the issuance of bonds (CHRAJ, 2017).

## Case 3: Conflict of Interest Allegation Against Dr Richard Anane (MP) and Minister of Roads and Transport

In 2005, the Commission on Human Rights and Administrative Justice investigated the Honourable Minister for Roads and Transport, Mr Richard Anane. The objective was to see if the Honourable Minister placed himself in a conflict of interest situation during the period under examination because of his relationship with a woman, Ms Alexandra O'Brien. The Minister was accused of transferring various sums of money to his mistress in the United States. The latter was also purporting to enter into a contract with the Ghanaian government (CHRAJ, 2005).

A conflict of interest, according to the Commission, occurs when a public official attempts to promote a private or personal interest for himself or another person, and the promotion of the private interest then results, is intended to result, appears to be, or has the potential to result in interference with the person's objective performance of his or her duties; and improper benefit or advantage by virtue of his/her position.

The Commission finds that the Respondent was in a conflict of interest situation as he began an intimate relationship after opening negotiations/discussions with Alexandra O'Brien. The latter was representing the World Health Monitor Programme (WHMP) in the said negotiations. WHMP was supposed to be negotiating with the Government of Ghana through the Ministry of Health's representative, the Respondent, to implement a programme that would help Ghana with diagnosis and data management to fight the HIV/AIDS scourge. The Honourable Minister was in a conflict of interest situation as he began an intimate relationship after he opened negotiations/discussions with Alexandra O'Brien, who was representing WHMP. The Commission recommends that the Minister be relieved of his post as Minister of State (CHRAJ, 2005).

## Case 4: Conflict of Interest and Bribery Allegation Against President Mahama on Ford Expedition Gift

In 2016, three different complaints were filed against President Mahama, alleging conflict of interest and bribery in connection with a Ford Expedition gift given to him by a Burkinabe contractor. The petitioners wanted CHRAJ to rule that President Mahama had violated Article 284 of the 1992 Constitution, which stipulates, "A public officer shall not place himself in a position where his personal interest interferes with or is likely to conflict with the discharge of the functions of his office."

The Commission looked at 13 issues, the most important of which was whether the President's acceptance of the Ford Expedition SUV violated the Code of Conduct for Public Officers' existing Gift Policy. Based on that broad guideline, the Commission expressed satisfaction that "the gift in question falls within the scope of gifts forbidden under the Gift Policy. Even though the Respondent later surrendered the gift to the State, the action was still in violation of the Gift Policy."

On the specific objective, whether the President's acceptance of the gift constituted a conflict of interest under the Code of Conduct for Public Officers and Conflict of Interest Rules. CHRAJ found that "the evidence available shows that, although the gift was offered to the respondent as a personal gift, the respondent surrendered the vehicle to be added to the Presidential pool as state property." The Commission further noted, "disclosure and surrendering of the gift are some of the ways prescribed under the guidelines for dealing with conflict of interest that may arise from gifts received in violation of the Gift Policy."

Although there are several instances of reported cases of conflicts of interest in Ghana, the above cases are few examples of high-level conflict of interest cases investigated by a constitutionally mandated body—CHRAJ (Graphic Online, 2016). The high number of reported cases could be attributed to a vibrant media supported by press freedom in Ghana.

# Some Conflict of Interest Situations in South Africa

## Case 1: Conflict of Interest Against Karen Killian (Employee) by Browns, The Diamond Store (Employer)

The employee, a sales consultant for the applicant (Browns, The Diamond Store), was fired after being found guilty of conflict of interest on 22 January 2013. The decision was based on a portion of the employee's contract, which states that "during the term of this agreement and thereafter, the employee will not use any confidential matter or information relating to the company's business affairs, processes, techniques, trade secrets, customers, and/or trade connections for her own benefit or the benefit of any other person, business, or entity, except as may be agreed upon".

The employer alleged that the employee provided some advice to her partner (a jewellery dealer) business including on how his employees should dress. The Labour Court of SA dismissed the case stating that employer did not provide any evidence of how the employee compromised its business. "For a conflict of interest to exist, the applicant must have acted against the respondent's interests. This could include disclosing the respondent's company processes or any other confidential information in order to promote her partner's business." (SAFLII, 2013).

## Case 2: Conflict of Interest Case Between Andre Herholdt and Nedbank Ltd and Congress of SA Trade Unions

Mr Andre Herholdt, a financial adviser at Nedbank Limited, was dismissed for failure to disclose a conflict of interest resulting from his appointment as a beneficiary in the will of a client, Mr John Smith. In

2007, Mr Herholdt was appointed by Mr Smith as a legatee to an amount of £92,000 investment, and as a life partner and sole successor to Mr Smith's inheritance in 2008. As required by Nedbank's conflict of interest policy, neither will was disclosed to Mr Herholdt's line manager.

He successfully challenged his dismissal in arbitration proceedings which was upheld by the Labour Court and Supreme Court of Appeal. The Labour Court and the Labour Appeal Court (LAC) held that "the only inference that could be drawn from the evidence was that Mr Herholdt deliberately chose not to disclose the existence of the two wills to his employer when he knew that he was obliged to do so. As he had not said why he did this, preferring to advance several spurious excuses, including the proposition that the wills did not give rise to a conflict of interest between the bank and its customer and that he was not aware of the obligation to disclose, their conclusion was that his non-disclosure was dishonest." (SAFLII, 2016).

# Some Conflict of Interest Cases from Kenya

## Case 1: Conflict of Interest—The Case of State Officers

The Office of the Director of Public Prosecutions filed an application in Constitutional Petition No. 204 of 2019 seeking orders prohibiting Honourable Senator James Aggrey Bob Orengo or any other state officer from appearing on behalf of the Petitioner or any of the parties in the case because of a conflict of interest. The core of the applicant's case was that Senator James Aggrey Bob Orengo is a full-time state officer who is prohibited by law from engaging in any other lucrative occupation because he is the elected Senator of Siaya County and the Minority Leader of the Senate. Though he has the right to practise law, he must not do so at the expense of the public interest.

On 27 April 2021, the court agreed with the Applicant that there was a conflict of interest in the circumstances and ordered the Petitioner to hire a lawyer other than Honourable Senator James Aggrey Bob Orengo. This implies that a state officer is barred from engaging in gainful employment in instances of conflict of interest or perception of it (Saroni & Stevens Advocates, 2021).

## Case 2: Conflict of Interest Case Against MOSES Kasaine Lenokulal and Orxy Service Station by Ethics and Anti-Corruption Commission

The application is based on preliminary findings by the petitioner that multiple companies that tendered and that were awarded high-value contracts by the county government between January 2013 and December 2018 were owned by county government personnel. This created a conflict of interest as defined by Section 2 of the Public Officer Ethics Act, resulting in a loss of $673 million for the county government. It further stated that during the same period when the first respondent was a governor, a business owned by him was awarded a contract to supply diesel/petrol. The first respondent, as a public officer as defined by Section 2 of the Public Office Ethics Act, was in a fiduciary position and thus in conflict of his personal and public interests when trading with the Samburu county government through the second respondent (Kenya Law, 2019).

# Discussion, Implications and Recommendations

The few scenarios of conflict of interest situations presented above, demonstrates the gravity of conflict of interest in public sector organisations in Africa and its linkage with corruption. It also suggests that there is an urgent need for effective strategies to deal with the canker in the sub-region. The following are some strategies that have been used as approaches to managing conflict of interest in the past decades. *Divestment of relevant public interest*: with this approach, the official's private interest (e.g. asset) can be divested (removed or sold) to prevent the official's private interest from influencing their official action (OECD, 2006; Vanagas & Juškys, 2019). Though it is practical to do so and likely to be acknowledged as appropriate by the public, both the official and their organisation must demonstrate clearly and openly that the official's interests were at arm's length from official actions and decisions in which they were involved. This is to ensure that public trust is not jeopardised (OECD, 2006).

*Recusal arrangements*: The public official withdraws from performing an official duty or participating in decision-making because of continuing ownership or control of relevant private interest. Recusal (withdrawal) can be used to handle a conflict of interest by having another official temporarily execute the tasks and responsibilities that would otherwise be (Vanagas & Juškys, 2019) affected by the conflict. This technique may not be effective in circumstances where the conflict of interest concerns a family, ethnicity, or religious affiliation (if the same conflict of interest is likely to occur often) (Ofori-Mensah, 2011; Vanagas & Juškys, 2019; Wu & Sun, 2014). Though these approaches have produced some level of effectiveness in dealing with conflict of interest, the increasing situations of conflict of interest have led some scholars and practitioners (e.g. Vanagas & Juškys, 2019) calling for a more effective approach to dealing with the menace. Based on these calls and suggestions, the authors of this chapter recommends the use of social marketing, which is a voluntary behaviour change technique as an approach to dealing with the menace of conflict of interest in public sector organisations in Africa.

## Addressing Conflict of Interest from a Social Marketing Perspective

As suggested by Vanagas and Juškys (2019), the fundamental goal of an effective conflict of interest policy is not to simply bar public officials from engaging in any private-capacity interests, even if such an approach were practicable. The immediate objective should be to maintain the integrity of official policy and administrative decisions and public management generally, recognising that an unresolved conflict of interest may result in abuse of public office. In other words, using policies, regulations, and enforcement alone might not be sufficient in the fight against conflict of interest. Scholars (e.g. Ayee, 2008) have noted that the increasing use of ethical codes and regulations, particularly in Africa where unethical behaviour has been the hallmark of public service, has produced little result in the fight against conflict of interest and related corrupt behaviours.

A rigorous approach to controlling the exercise of private interests may collide with other rights, be ineffective or counterproductive in practice, or deter some people from running for public office (Ochoa & Graycar, 2016; Vanagas & Juškys, 2019; World Bank, 2012). Other scholars such as Serfontein and de Waal (2015) have also suggested a move that will go beyond legislation and enforcement and incorporate a significant education element for government employees on their responsibility to act in the public interest. Research has, however, shown that public education and awareness programmes only make people aware of a situation or condition but make little impact in terms of influencing behaviour (Madill & Abele, 2007; Serfontein & de Waal, 2015). Despite the noted limitations of the traditional approach of using ethical codes and regulations, little effort is made towards using other approaches such as behavioural change approaches.

According to Serfontein and de Waal (2015), initiatives seeking to invoke voluntary willingness of public officials to maintain the integrity of their decisions will be an effective means to deal with the canker of conflict of interest. Based on these assertions, the authors posit that though the traditional approach to managing conflict of interest has made some strides, dealing with the situation from a behavioural change perspective using social marketing approach will contribute significantly to the fight against conflict of interest in the Ghanaian public sector.

Social marketing is applying marketing principles and techniques alongside other principles to influence the target audience to voluntarily reject or adopt a new behaviour for the benefit of society and the individual. The social marketing concept has been used in several instances. It has been proven to be an effective means of solving most societal problems, such as changing behaviour towards waste management (Tweneboah-Koduah et al., 2020) alcohol abuse (Wettstein et al., 2012) and so on.

Realising the need for voluntary commitment and change in behaviour towards conflict of interest situations, CHRAJ called for a two-month training for all public officials and elected or appointed officials. In line with this realisation, the Commission further established a Human Rights Training Manual for Teachers, which includes anti-corruption education, as part of initiatives to instil integrity in the younger generation and support the teaching of anti-corruption as part of human rights education.

## Conclusion

The chapter sought to examine the fundamental issues of conflict of interest and of how they affect public sector institutions in Ghana. The chapter reveals that conflict of interest could lead to corruption if not adequately identified and addressed. Thus, preventing a conflict of interest is likely to reduce corruption to the barest minimum in Sub-Saharan Africa, including Ghana. The study further shows that past and present governments in Ghana have made several efforts to address the conflict of interest canker. Some of these efforts include the establishment of CHRAJ with a core mandate to investigate conflict of interest and abuse of public office, the Public Office Holding Act to ensure that public officers declare their assets before assuming office, and after every four years. Despite these efforts, studies have shown that the conflict of interest remains a bane in public institutions in Ghana. In other words, little has been achieved in the fight against conflict of interest in Ghana despite the various efforts to address it. Based on this assertion, the chapter recommends using behavioural change approaches that use marketing principles and techniques to design effective interventions that seek to elicit voluntary change in attitude towards the menace of conflict of interest.

## References

Ayee, J. R. (2008). *Reforming the African public sector: Retrospect and prospects.* The CODESRIA.

Catchick, P. (2014). Conflict of interest: Gateway to corruption. *ACFE European Fraud Conference, 23*(4), 412–422.

CHRAJ. (2005). *In the matter of the Commission on Human Rights and Administrative Justice Act, 1993 (Act 456).*

CHRAJ. (2017). *Decision on Ken Ofori-Atta's bond issued.* https://chraj.gov.gh/wp-content/uploads/2018/06/DECISION-ON-KEN-OFORI-ATTAS-BONDS-ISSUED.pdf

Citinewsroom. (2020). *Suspended CEO of PPA guilty of conflict of interest; unfit for any public office—CHRAJ.* https://citinewsroom.com/2020/10/suspended-ppa-ceo-guilty-of-conflict-of-interest-unfit-for-any-public-office-chraj/

Graphic Online. (2016). *CHRAJ clears Mahama of bribery allegation on ford (FULL DOCUMENT).* https://www.graphic.com.gh/news/general-news/how-chraj-dismissed-bribery-allegations-against-prez-mahama.html

Graphic Online. (2020). *A former head of CHRAJ has called for a behavioral change approach to dealing with conflict of interest and a legislation that clearly define it.* https://www.graphic.com.gh/news/politics/ghana-news-conflict-of-interest-not-defined-in-constitution-emile-short.html

Graphic Online. (2021). *Conduct of public officers bill, 2013.* https://www.graphic.com.gh/news/general-news/conduct-of-public-officers-bill-passed-by-parliament.html

IEA. (2016). *The role of assets declaration regime.* The Institute of Economic Affairs (Issue 44).

Katee, A. (2017). Rethinking the conflict of interest policy in Kenya. *International Journal of Law, Humanities & Social Science, 1*(2), 58–63.

Kenya Law. (2019). *Ethics and anti-corruption commission v Moses Kasaine Lenokulal & another.* http://kenyalaw.org/caselaw/cases/view/180057/

Madill, J., & Abele, F. (2007). From public education to social marketing: The evolution of the Canadian heritage anti-racism social marketing program. *Journal of Nonprofit & Public Sector Marketing, 17*(1–2), 27–53.

Mafunisa, J. J. (2003). Conflict of interest: Ethical dilemma in politics and administration. *South African Journal of Labour Relations, 27*(2), 4–22.

Munzhedzi, P. H. (2016). South African public sector procurement and corruption: Inseparable twins? *Journal of Transport and Supply Chain Management, 13*(5), 1–8.

Ochoa, R., & Graycar, A. (2016). Tackling conflicts of interest: Policy instruments in different settings. *Public Integrity, 18*(1), 83–100.

Odoi, R. N. I. I. (2021). *The commission on human rights and administrative justice of Ghana in retrospect.* Available at SSRN 3825712, 1–46.

OECD. (2006). Managing conflict of interest in the public sector: A toolkit. In *Managing conflict of interest in the public sector.* OECD Publishing.

Ofori-Mensah, M. (2011). Regulating conflicts of interest: Could do better? *The Institute of Economic Affairs, 17*(2), 1–8.

Osei-Tutu, E., Offei-Nyarko, K., Ameyaw, C., & Twumasi-Ampofo, K. (2014). Conflict of interest and related corrupt practices in public procurement in Ghana. *International Journal of Civil Engineering Construction and Estate Management, 1*(2), 1–15.

Rahman, K. (2018). Overview of corruption and anti-corruption in Ghana. *Transparency International (The Global Coalition Against Corruption), 6*(3), 1–18.

SAFLII. (2013). *Conflict of interest case between Andre Herholdt and Nedbank Ltd and Congress of SA Trade Unions.* South African Legal Information Institute. http://www.saflii.org/za/cases/ZASCA/2013/97.html

SAFLII. (2016). *Browns the Diamond Store v Commission for Conciliation, Mediation and Arbitration and others (JR1172/14).* South African Legal Information Institute. http://www.saflii.org/za/cases/ZALCJHB/2016/187.html

Saroni & Stevens Advocates. (2021). *Conflict of interest—The case of state officers.* Newsletter, American Marketing Association. http://saronistevens.co.ke/2021/04/29/conflict-of-interest-the-case-of-state-officers/

Serfontein, E., & de Waal, E. (2015). The corruption bogey in South Africa: Is public education safe? *South African Journal of Education, 35*(1), 1–12.

Spence, E. (2004). Conflicts of interest and corruption. *Australian Journal of Professional and Applied Ethics, 5*(2), 25–36.

Tweneboah-Koduah, E. Y., Adams, M., & Nyarku, K. M. (2020). Using theory in social marketing to predict waste disposal behaviour among households in Ghana. *Journal of African Business, 21*(1), 62–77.

Vanagas, R., & Juškys, A. (2019). Management of conflict of interest in the public sector in Lithuania: Theory and practice. *Contemporary Research on Organization Management and Administration, 5*(1), 6–21.

Wettstein, D., Suggs, L. S., & Lellig, C. (2012). Social marketing and alcohol misuse prevention in German-speaking countries. *Journal of Social Marketing, 2*(3), 187–206.

World Bank. (2012). *Identifying and managing conflicts of interest in the public sector: Good practice guide.*

Wu, H., & Sun, X. (2014). Managing conflicts of interest in China's public sector: Fighting corruption at the early stage. *Richmond Journal of Global Law and Business, 13*(1), 145.

Yeboah-Assiamah, E., Asamoah, K., Bawole, J. N., & Musah-Surugu, I. J. (2016). A socio-cultural approach to public sector corruption in Africa: Key pointers for reflection. *Journal of Public Affairs, 16*(3), 279–293.

# 4

# The Subversion of the South African Public Accountability Ethics Codes of Conduct in the Name of Disaster Management During COVID-19 Pandemic

Mpfareleni Mavis Netswera and Fulufhelo Netswera

## Introduction

Ethics can be defined as being concerned with how human beings should live their lives. Ethics has to do with what is right and wrong, fair or unfair, caring or uncaring, good or bad, responsible or irresponsible. Further, the view on ethics includes the principles, the norms and standards of conduct governing individuals or groups. Within the realm of public service, ethics is concerned with the application of morality, based

M. M. Netswera (✉)
University of South Africa (UNISA), Pretoria, South Africa
e-mail: netswmm@unisa.ac.za

F. Netswera
Durban University of Technology, Durban, South Africa
e-mail: Fulufhelon@dut.ac.za

© The Author(s), under exclusive license to Springer Nature Switzerland AG 2022
K. Ogunyemi et al. (eds.), *Ethics and Accountable Governance in Africa's Public Sector,*
*Volume I*, Palgrave Studies of Public Sector Management in Africa,
https://doi.org/10.1007/978-3-030-95394-2_4

on what the public officials do, and how they do it. Being responsible for your action in the public service is therefore judged as ethically proper or accountable to the public (Brauns & Mdlazi, 2015). Examples of immoral behaviour include corruption, which is defined as an abuse of public positions for personal gain. At times, such behaviour does not benefit the perpetrator personally but can be for the benefit of one's political party, class, friends and family. The first act of corruption involves the abuse of office by low and middle level bureaucrats in discharging their daily tasks wherein they solicit bribes and other benefits from ordinary citizens. The grand corruption, which is the focus of the article's deliberation, involves high level government officials who at times take advantage of the weaknesses in the state's institutional frameworks for their personal benefits (Rakolobe, 2019).

On 5 January 2020, the World Health Organisation (WHO) published a report about the new deadly disease called coronavirus, later to be popularly known as COVID-19. In the wake of the coronavirus outbreak, South Africa, like many other countries, decided to take urgent and drastic measures to manage the disease and protect their citizens. By 15 March 2020, 61 individuals had tested positive for COVID-19 in South Africa. As President Cyril Ramaphosa announced, 'We have now declared a national state of disaster in terms of the Disaster Management Act. This will enable us to have an integrated and coordinated disaster management mechanism that will focus on preventing and reducing the outbreak of this virus' (Ramaphosa, 2020a).

The drastic measures taken to curb the spread of infections included closing schools, instituting travel restrictions, banning the sale of alcohol and tobacco and mandating compulsory wearing of face masks and sanitising hands at public places. On his second COVID-19 media briefing to the nation, President Ramaphosa announced that the state would introduce a fiscal package to support various sectors of the economy (Ramaphosa, 2020b). These measures included tax relief, disaster relief funds, emergency procurement of Personal Protective Equipment (PPE), wage support through the Unemployment Insurance Fund (UIF) and funding of ailing small businesses. It was a massive social relief, an economic stimulus package worth R500 billion estimated to be nearly 10% of the Gross Domestic Product (GDP) (Ramaphosa, 2020b).

A few months after President Ramaphosa's R500 billion COVID-19 relief package announcement, he signed a proclamation that allowed the Special Investigating Unit (SIU) to probe allegations of corruption and fraud. The trail of COVID-19 procurement corruption incidents is equally astonishing and estimated at R14 billion (Chelin, 2021). Claims on popular media were already making headlines suggesting that in the face of the unfolding health crisis, there were individuals who were massively defrauding the state. Government officials and mainly those in the health departments at both national and provincial governments were alleged to have been allotting tenders to politically connected individuals, including their family members and friends (Phakathi, 2020).

Most African countries are generally ranked poorly in global corruption perception indexes in general (Olken & Pande, 2012). The health sector is often singled out with concerns given how corruption hampers access to, and utilisation of health services. In the Anglophone West African countries of Gambia, Ghana, Liberia, Nigeria and Sierra Leone, corruption has been linked to many adverse outcomes, including reduced efficiency of health systems and increased mortality, due to inappropriate procurement and theft of medical supplies (Onwujekwe et al., 2019).

Ethics can be defined as the norm or standards concerned with how human beings should fairly conduct themselves. It has to do with what is right and wrong, fair or unfair, caring or uncaring, good or bad, responsible or irresponsible. Further, the view on ethics includes the principles, the norms and standards of conduct governing individuals or groups. Within the realm of public service, ethics is concerned with the application of morality, based on what the public officials do, and how they do it. Being responsible for your action in the public service is therefore judged as ethically proper or accountable to the public (Brauns & Mdlazi, 2015). Examples of immoral behaviour include corruption, which is defined as an abuse of public positions for personal gain. At times, such behaviour does not benefit the perpetrator personally but can be for the benefit of their political party, class, friends and family. The first act of corruption involves the abuse of office by low and middle level bureaucrats in discharging their daily tasks wherein they solicit bribes and other benefits from ordinary citizens. The grand corruption, which is the focus of this chapter's deliberation, involves high level government officials who at times take advantage of the weaknesses in the state's institutional frameworks for their personal benefits (Rakolobe, 2019).

In the context of the COVID-19 challenges and associated public sector corruption, this chapter attempts to determine how the executive code of ethics and the public service code of conduct were trumped. The chapter also refers to how other African countries confronted and managed corruption amidst mega-disasters such as Ebola (West Africa) and flooding outbreaks (Mozambique). The chapter is structured to engage the following themes: the management of disasters internationally, the importance of the code of ethics and public service code of conduct in curbing corruption in the public service, emergency procurement in response to the COVID-19 pandemic and a case of COVID-19 PPE corruption in the South African public service.

# The Management of Disasters Internationally

Disaster management fundamentally "deals with management of resources and information towards a disastrous event and is measured by how efficiently, effectively and seamlessly one coordinates these resources" (Modh, 2010). Catastrophes, either natural or disease, have devastating consequences. They take lives, and destroy infrastructure and nature itself. For example, in the Southern African state of Mozambique, the two worst floods of 2000 and 2001 affected up to four and a half million people (Foley, 2007). The earthquake and tsunami that hit the Indian Ocean in 2004 killed at least 200,000 people. This natural disaster killed more people than any other tsunami in recorded history. It is considered the third-largest earthquake in the world since 1900. The Ebola virus outbreak in West Africa in 2014 is considered the largest breakout ever (Luz, 2021; Duri, 2021).

These calamities required immediate relief involving a wide range of actors including the government, civil society, international organisations and media. Huge sums of money are availed to address major catastrophes of this nature for emergency procurement of goods and services. A possible outcome is that any humanitarian crisis becomes an opportunity for corruption.

- Put public interest first in the execution of their duties,
- Refrain from favouring relatives and friends in work-related activities,
- Be honest and accountable in handling public funds and use public service property and other resources only for authorised official purposes,
- Not use official positions to obtain private gifts or benefits during the performance of official duties nor accept any gifts or benefits when offered, as these may be construed as bribes (Office of the Public Service Commission, 1997).

There is an anticipation that compliance with the Code of Conduct will enhance professionalism and improve confidence in the Public Service. The question revolves around adherence to the Code, its effectiveness in promoting good behaviour and curbing corruption and the consequences for disobedience. In November 2018, the Public Service Commission (PSC), mandated to promote the values and principles governing public administration reported that, between 2004 and 2018, it generated 20,726 corruption cases in the public service through the national anti-corruption hotline (Nkosi, 2018). These are corruption cases related to social grant fraud, appointment irregularities, unethical behaviour, bribery and procurement irregularities. During the same period, 1740 officials were dismissed from the public service. Another 450 officials were fined while 140 officials were demoted. A further 927 officials were given final written warnings while 395 officials were prosecuted. The utilisation of the national anti-corruption hotline is deemed effective, though data is sketchy about the amount of public funds that is lost or recovered during these transgressions (Nkosi, 2018; SAnews, 2018).

It is estimated that corruption that took place during the period 2008–2016, that is, under the Presidency of Mr Jacob Zuma cost South Africa between R1 trillion and R4.9 trillion (Mnganga-Gcabashe, 2018; Merten, 2019; Sabcnews, 2019). By the end of 2018, corruption had brought such state-owned enterprises as Eskom, South African Airways (SAA), Transnet and the South African Broadcasting Authority (SABC) to their knees (Sabcnews, 2019). The CPI, which scores 180 countries worldwide through perceived levels of public sector corruption, scored South Africa 44 (2020) down from 56 (2010). Unfortunately, Sub-Saharan Africa is the lowest-scoring region with an average of 32. The Index further held that regional leaders have a tendency of utilising state funds to win elections, consolidate power and further personal interests. Botswana is the beacon of hope in the region though, with a score of 61(Transparency International, 2020). In Lesotho, the level of corruption seems to be on the decline in recent years. However, it is argued that the highly politicised public service contributes to the corruption scourge that is besieging the mountainous kingdom that is surrounded by South Africa (Rakolobe, 2019). The CPI recommends that to end corruption, "governments should reduce the risk of undue influence in policy-making by tightening controls over financial and other interests of government officials" (Transparency International, 2020).

To examine the adherence to Code of Ethics by legislatures and the executive in South Africa, the Joint Committee on Ethics and Members' Interests annually releases the Register of Members' Declaration of Interests. Annually, some members fail to declare their financial benefits to Parliament. Others have been accused of not disclosing certain financial benefits to Parliament, including President Ramaphosa (Umraw, 2019). The Public Protector found that while he was the Deputy President of the country, he breached the Ethical Conduct by not declaring financial benefits received towards his presidential campaign (Public Protector, 2019). The Economic Freedom Fighters (EFF) leader Julius Malema and his deputy Floyd Shivambu are also alleged to have failed to declare some financial benefits to Parliament (Constitutionally Speaking, 2019). Since 1994, Mr Tony Yengeni, however, remains the only member ever convicted of fraud and sent to jail for failing to declare a financial benefit to Parliament. It is essential to note that there are a handful of parliamentary members who are presently facing corruption charges in parliament and from their political party (Parliament of South Africa, 2021; De Vos, 2019).

While there is no one-size-fits-all approach to curbing public service corruption, factors contributing to the overall effectiveness of the Code of Conduct include the mechanisms available for reporting and addressing actual and potential offences for example, hotlines and protection of whistle-blowers. There must also be sanctions for violations; otherwise, a code becomes toothless (Nagiah, 2012).

# COVID-19 Emergency Procurement Aligned to the Disaster Management Act 57 of 2002

Designated under Section 3 of the Disaster Management Act 57 of 2002, the Minister of Cooperative Governance and Traditional Affairs (COGTA), Dr Nkosazana Dlamini Zuma, declared a national state of disaster on 15 March 2020. In terms of Section 27(1) of the Act, the Minister of COGTA may declare a national state of disaster after having recognised the existence of special circumstances to warrant such declaration (Cooperative Governance and Traditional Affairs, 2020a; South Africa, 2002).

Subsequently, the Minister issued regulations regarding steps necessary to alleviate, contain and minimise the effect of COVID-19. The regulations provided matters related to the release of resources for the duration of the declared national state of disaster, prevention and prohibition of gatherings, limitation on the sale, dispensing or transportation of liquor, closure of school, emergency procurement procedures to name a few (Cooperative Governance and Traditional Affairs, 2020b).

Simultaneously, the National Treasury issued an instruction note in terms of Section 76(4)(g) of the Public Finance Management Act 1 of 1999 (PFMA) to allow for the relaxation, to a certain extent, of supply chain management requirements during the emergency time to expedite procurement (South Africa, 1999). The Instruction Note aimed to augment and enhance uniformity across all organs of state. The Note lists prices of goods/commodities in efforts to curb opportunistic use of COVID-19 to escalate profit margins. An annexure of the list of available goods/commodities and items not catered for on the Transversal Contracts but can be procured from an enclosed list of compliant service providers was provided. This Instruction Note was aligned to a Circular issued by the Department of Public Service and Administration giving guidelines for the containment and management of COVID-19 in the public service (National Treasury South Africa, 2020).

Since late March 2020, the country has been on an extended nationwide lockdown under different alert levels. Alert levels determine the stages of restrictions applied nationwide. Alert Level 1 indicates a low COVID-19 spread with a high health system readiness and Alert Level 5 indicates the highest COVID-19 spread with a low health system readiness (Government of South Africa, 2020) (Table 4.1).

On 25 June 2021, the acting Minister of Health reported 1,877,143 laboratory-confirmed COVID-19 cases and 59,406 fatalities from March 2020 to June 2021. The country has thus far administered Pfizer and Johnson & Johnson vaccines to no fewer than 2,500,000 people or less than 4% of the population. During the third week of June 2021, the country entered a third wave. There are now demands by the public to fast-track the rollout of vaccines (Kubayi, 2021). Worldwide, the WHO has admitted the imbalance in the distribution of vaccines with most COVID-19 vaccines having been administered in wealthy nations. On average, almost one in four people residing in high-income countries have by June 2021 received a jab as against one in more than 500 in low-income countries (United Nations, 2021).

Table 4.1  Summary of lockdown alert levels, South Africa

| Alert level 5 | Alert level 4 | Alert level 3 | Alert level 2 | Alert level 1 |
|---|---|---|---|---|
| Objective | | | | |
| Drastic measures to contain the spread of the virus and save lives | Extreme precautions to limit community transmission and outbreaks, while allowing some activity to resume | Restrictions on many activities, including at workplaces and socially to address a high risk of transmission | Physical distancing and restrictions on leisure and social activities to prevent a resurgence of the virus | Most normal activity can resume, with precautions and health guidelines followed at all times. Population prepare for an increase in alert levels if necessary |

Source: Government of South Africa (2020)

# A Case of COVID-19 PPE Procurement Corruption in South Africa's Public Sector

In times of disasters, emergency procurement attracts large and unprecedented economic stimulus packages, to stimulate economic recovery and growth. Within the first half of 2020, COVID-19 programmes amounted to between 10% and 20% of GDP in countries such as Germany, Japan, South Africa and the United States of America (Oldfield, 2020; Duri, 2021). Germany approved the largest stimulus programme in Europe encompassing a fiscal impulse worth almost €500 billion and other financial support worth billions of euros in grants to small businesses. South Africa's economic stimulus programme amounted to US$25 billion or roughly 10% of GDP. In Japan, three rounds of economic stimulus programme were announced to a total of US$2.18 trillion. Likewise, the USA set aside a US$2.2 trillion stimulus programme to recuperate the country's economy (Oldfield, 2020).

The South African government allocated a R500 billion COVID-19 stimulus package which translated to 10% of the GDP. Of this amount, R270 billion was for tax relief and credit guarantees for bank loans to businesses in distress. The remaining R230 billion was for relief to individuals, households and businesses (Auditor General of South Africa, 2020). As a share of GDP, South Africa's COVID-19 package represents the largest in the low-income countries and notably larger than several high-income countries, including South Korea and Canada. However, such a package has come at the expense of a massive rise in the fiscal deficit from 6.7% of GDP in 2019/2020 to 14% in 2020/2021 (Planting, 2021). The challenge for the government and policymakers is to find instruments on both the revenue collection and expenditure sides to place the country on a measured and optimal fiscal consolidation path (Bhorat & Köhler, 2020) (Fig. 4.1).

In the dramatic turn of events, the National Treasury issued an instruction to government departments across all three spheres to halt the emergency procurement of COVID-19 PPE due to suspected corruption in August 2020 (Mothibi, 2021a). Prominent public figures who have since resigned, suspended or fired for PPE corruption include Dr Bandile Masuku (Gauteng provincial political head for health), his wife and the

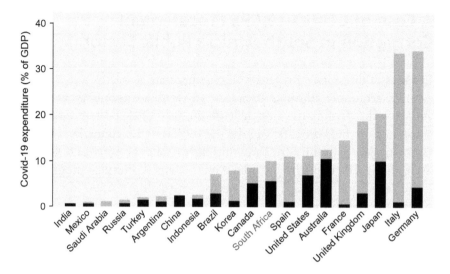

**Fig. 4.1** COVID-19 stimulus expenditure by country (% of GDP). (Source: Bhorat & Köhler, 2020)

former presidential spokesperson Ms Khusela Diko for a PPE tender worth R125 million (Stephen, 2021). Dr Zweli Mkhize the country's Health Minister is on suspension over a PPE tender worth R150 million. A R10 million scooter ambulance tender awarded to Fabkomp (Pty) Ltd by the now dismissed head of health department in the Eastern Cape Province, Sindiswa Gomba has also been declared unlawful by the SIU (E-news Channel Africa, 2021).

In the first special COVID-19 relief package report, the now late Auditor General Kimi Makwetu, reported that the funds landed in an environment with many control weaknesses. In essence, his views were that public accountability was in crisis. He remarked that "emergency responses and quick actions are required to save lives and livelihoods, but the easing of controls and the streamlining of processes and procedures to respond to the crisis expose the government to the risks of the misuse or abuse of public resources" (Makwetu, 2020, pp. 1–2).

The present Auditor General Tsakani Maluleke further reported significant deficiencies in the procurement and contract management of the COVID-19 relief package such as support to vulnerable households, wage protection, healthcare services and basic education but applauded the government's ongoing efforts in fighting the pandemic (Auditor General, 2020). The real-time audit report on the government's COVID-19 expenditure on PPE discovered that the bulk of the government's procurement of PPE took place in the health and education sectors, with an estimated R4.6 billion spent by 30 September 2020 (Maluleke, 2020). The PPE sample of contracts and transactions audited, focused on those that displayed certain risk indicators and revealed the following key findings:

- There were instances where competitive processes were not followed, resulting in the contract being awarded to a specific supplier or group of suppliers without the necessary motivation or approval for such deviations;
- The National Treasury standing requirement to favour local producers was not applied consistently in all the PPE procurement processes;
- The importance of ensuring that suppliers' tax affairs are in order fell by the wayside for many of the PPE contracts awarded;
- Businesses that provide PPE across the country were not treated in a fair and equal manner, as some were disqualified based on not complying with the requirements, while others were not; and
- In various instances, contracts were awarded to businesses that do not have a history of providing PPE—often working in a different industry or even being formed or registered just before contracts are awarded (Maluleke, 2020).

In this regard, the AG's concern is not just about legislative compliance, but also about the fairness in selection and the ability of such businesses to deliver on the PPE contracts (Maluleke, 2020). In terms of quality, price and delivery of PPE, the AG audit found prevalence of procurement at prices higher than the market rates. Some suppliers delivered PPE which did not meet the minimum required specifications nor deliver what they had been contracted to deliver or under-delivered or delivered late. Despite this, the suppliers were still paid (Maluleke, 2020).

The extent of the deficiencies in the procurement of the COVID-19 relief package is explicitly exposed in the SIU's probe into allegations on the PPE procurement by state institutions. Through this enquiry, the SIU investigated allegations on the procurement of goods and services. The SIU further instituted civil proceedings in the Special Tribunal for the recovery of losses or the prevention of further losses against some contracted companies (Mothibi, 2021a).

The head of the SIU, Advocate Andy Mothibi, reported that between April 2020 and March 2021, total COVID-19 expenditure was R126.7 billion. Out of that expenditure, R14.3 billion is under investigation by the SIU. The number of PPE contracts awarded for COVID-19 related services under investigation by the SIU is 4117. These contracts were awarded to 2251 service providers. The finalised investigations at the point of this publication were 40% from whom R600 million had been recovered. Additionally, 54% are currently being assessed and 6% were yet to start. More allegations were still surfacing and received by the SIU. As a result, the number of cases keep on changing from one progress report to the next (Mothibi, 2021b; Parliamentary Monitoring Group, 2021) (Table 4.2).

Observations of COVID-19 contract inquiries have noted a high prevalence of fraud and corruption including non-compliance with minimum emergency prescripts that guarantee fairness, equitable, transparent, competitive and cost-effective (Mothibi, 2021a). Further, non-adherence to product specifications and purchase of substandard products not suitable for intended purposes were found. Some service providers were only registered a few days before they were contracted to provide services and thus have no demonstrable track records. In some instances, political pressure played a role in PPE procurement decisions as reported in Reuters (2021). The impression is that the names of the service providers were determined before any procurement process commenced. There was not even an attempt to negotiate with suppliers in bringing prices within the thresholds provided by the National Treasury Note. This resulted in overpayment for goods. In summary, government institutions lacked basic control measures to ensure that payments were only made for goods and services that were delivered at the right price and quality (Mothibi, 2021a). The value and details of the matters that were brought before the Special Tribunal by December 2020 are as follows (Table 4.3).

By June 2021, an update on the SIU probe provided additional referrals for disciplinary action against officials and new referrals to the

**Table 4.2** Current status of investigations

| Contracts investigation status | No of service providers | No of contracts awarded to service providers | Value of contracts awarded | Per cent value of cases under investigation |
|---|---|---|---|---|
| Summary of progress as of 30 April 2021 | | | | |
| Finalised | 835 | 1071 | R5,736,906,649 | 40% |
| Ongoing | 1084 | 2695 | R7,670,305,352 | 54% |
| Yet to commence | 332 | 351 | R878,888,474 | 6% |
| **Total** | 2251 | 4117 | R14,286,100,475 | 100% |

| Outcome achieved | Number | Value |
|---|---|---|
| Summary of outcomes achieved between 23 July 2020 and 25 November 2020 | | |
| Rand value of potential cash and/or assets to be recovered | – | R160,647,890 |
| Rand value of actual cash and/or assets recovered (4 February 2021) | – | R127,220,543 |
| Number of referrals made for disciplinary action against officials (December 2020) | 25 | - |
| Number of referrals made for executive and/or administrative action | 2 | - |
| The number of referrals made to the relevant prosecuting authorities | 38 | - |
| Rand value of matters in respect of which evidence was referred for the institution or defence/opposition of civil proceedings | – | R259,624,735 |

Adapted from: Mothibi (2021a, 2021b)

relevant prosecuting authority. A Digital Vibes contract worth R150 million is equally under investigation for irregular procurement and implicates the Minister of Health who has since been placed under special leave (Parliamentary Monitoring Group, 2021; Mavuso, 2021).

# Conclusion and Recommendations

Emergency procurement is an international phenomenon that is meant to undo the effects of natural or medical disasters. However, the associated relief and services procurement are prone to massive corruption.

Table 4.3 Civil litigation cases instituted in the special tribunal

| Province | Description | Value of outcome | Progress to date |
|---|---|---|---|
| Eastern Cape | Department of Health: SIU v Fabkomp (Pty) (Ltd) and Others: (EC04/2020) | R10,148,750 | The cause of action is based on the irregular procurement by the Eastern Cape Department of Health of motorcycles with a "sidecar" to transport patients, which resulted in a process that was not fair, competitive or cost-effective |
| Eastern Cape | The OR Tambo Municipality "Door-to-door" case: (EC06/2020) | R4,899,000 | This matter relates to an investigation into the irregular procurement of COVID-19 awareness campaign that was conducted in the Eastern Cape while there was on a strict level 4 lockdown |
| Eastern Cape | The Alinani Trading-matter (EC05/2020) | R2,785,276 | This matter relates to the procurement of PPE for the Department of Education in the Eastern Cape |
| Gauteng | The SIU v Ledla Structural Development (Pty) Ltd and 43 Others: (GP07/2020) | R139,000,000 | In this matter, a contract to deliver PPE was irregularly awarded by the Gauteng Department of Health, while unit prices were also artificially inflated by between 211% and 542% |

(continued)

Table 4.3  (continued)

| Province | Description | Value of outcome | Progress to date |
|---|---|---|---|
| Gauteng | SIU v Kabelo Mantsu Lehloenya, Professor Mkhululi Lukhele and MEC for Gauteng Health (GP11/2020) | R43,532,709 | The SIU issued summons against three defendants, including a former Head of Department for the Department of Health and the MEC for Gauteng Health in which the SIU seeks to recover losses suffered by the Department |
| Kwazulu Natal | Department of Social Development: Rosette Investments (KN01/2020); Gibela (KN02/2020); LNA Communications (KN03/2020); Zain Brothers (KN04/2020) | R4,899,000 R4,899,000 R3,960,000 R4,800,000 | This matter relates to the irregular procurement of blankets for the Department of Social Development in KZN. The investigation revealed that, in fact, fewer blankets were distributed than the Department had in its stores prior to embarking on the procurement |
| Limpopo | National Department of Public Works and Infrastructure: The SIU v Caledon River Properties (Pty) (Ltd) and Others Beitbridge Border matter: (GP12/20 and LP01/2020) | R40,800,000 | This matter relates to the procurement of a service provider/contractor for the erection of a fence along the SA border with Zimbabwe, near Beitbridge. The SIU investigation found evidence that the procurement was irregular |

Source: Mothibi (2021a)

Because huge resources are overwhelmingly availed with demands for speedy disbursement, government officials often see an opportunity to enrich themselves, their families and friends. Disaster relief corruption is, therefore, an international phenomenon, though more pronounced in some countries than others are. Literature in this chapter on relief efforts for the Ebola struck West Africa or flooding and tsunami in Mozambique and Sri Lanka respectively show evidence of corruption.

COVID-19 remains an unfolding international medical catastrophe that has far-reaching consequences. Emerging evidence from across the world already suggests that there is an overwhelming breach of the code of ethics and codes of good conduct by public servants when it relates to COVID-19 procurement and relief efforts. The implications are both huge and dire with consequence for unnecessary and preventable deaths in favour of the enrichment of a few businesses and individuals closely associated with state officials.

The South African COVID-19 emergency stimulus package estimated at R500 billion which is nearly 10% of its annual GDP is alleged to be subject of massive COVID-19 procurement corruption estimated at nearly R14 billion. This massive looting of public resources happens despite clear guidelines for ethical conduct such as the Code of Ethics for parliamentarians and the Code for Good Conduct for public servants and the National Treasury directive for procurement under COVID-19 lockdown. Of importance, however, is not just the existence of laws and regulations to guide procurement but the enforcement of punitive measures among those who flout the regulations. It is therefore commendable that South Africa has taken a stance against COVID-19 procurement corruption by instituting investigations, some of which have resulted in arrests and recouping of funds. South Africa has, over the past decade, experienced massive public service corruption estimated at between R1 and R4.9 trillion. These COVID-19 investigations, the enforcement of the Code of Ethics and Code of Good Conduct, suspension and trial of public officials and recouping of corruption funds is seen as a turn of a new leaf in its fight against corruption.

# References

African Union. (2011). *African charter on values and principles of public service and administration.* Adopted by the 16th Ordinary Session of the Heads of State and Government of the AU Addis Ababa, Ethiopia—31st January 2011.

Agency for modernization, Local Government Denmark and Danish Regions. (2017). Code of conduct in the public sector. https://modst.dk/media/18742/code-of-conduct-in-the-public-sectorforside.pdf

Auditor General. (2020). *Second special report on the financial management of government's COVID-19 initiatives.* Auditor General.

Bak, M. (2020). *Mozambique: Overview of corruption and anti-corruption.* Transparency International.

Bhorat, H., & Köhler, T. (2020). Lockdown economics in South Africa: Social assistance and the Ramaphosa stimulus package. https://www.brookings.edu/blog/africa-in-focus/2020/11/20/lockdown-economics-in-south-africa-social-assistance-and-the-ramaphosa-stimulus-package/

Brauns, M., & Mdlazi, D. (2015). Ethics, codes of conduct, morals and professionalism as a bulwark against corruption and unethical conduct in the public sector: A case of South Africa.

Chelin, R. (2021). South Africa's mixed messages on procurement corruption. *Institute for Security Studies*, 11 October 2021. https://issafrica.org/iss-today/south-africas-mixed-messages-on-procurement-corruption

Constitutionally Speaking. (2019). Why more MPS who misled parliament have not been prosecuted for fraud. https://constitutionallyspeaking.co.za/why-more-mps-who-misled-parliament-have-not-been-prosecuted-for-fraud/

Cooperative Governance and Traditional Affairs. (2020a). *Declaration of a National State of Disaster.* Government Printers.

Cooperative Governance and Traditional Affairs. (2020b). *Regulations issued in terms of Section 27(2) of the Disaster Management Act, 2002.* Government Printers.

De Vos, P. (2019). Why more MPs who misled Parliament have not been prosecuted for fraud. https://www.dailymaverick.co.za/opinionista/2019-11-27-why-more-mps-who-misled-parliament-have-not-been-rosecuted-for-fraud/

Disasters Emergency Committee. (2001). Independent evaluation of expenditure of DEC Mozambique floods appeal funds: March to December 2000. : Valid International.

Duri, J. (2021). *Corruption in times of crisis.* Transparency International.

E-news Channel Africa. (2021). Mkhize's special leave welcomed. https://www.enca.com/news/zweli-mkhizes-special-leave-welcomed

Foley, C. (2007). *Mozambique: A case study in the role of the affected state in humanitarian action.* Humanitarian Policy Group Working Paper, Overseas Development Institute, London, UK.

Government of South Africa. (2020). About alert system. https://www.gov.za/COVID-19/about/about-alert-system

Kubayi, M. (2021). Coronavirus COVID-19 and vaccination rollout programme. https://www.gov.za/speeches/minister-mmamoloko-kubayi-coronavirus-COVID-19-and-vaccination-rollout-plan-25-jun-2021

Luz, A. O. S. (2021). *Emergencies: Increasing the opportunities to corruption?* Geneva Global Policy Brief No 1/2021, 1–8.

Makwetu, K. (2020). *Auditor-General says the multi-billion-rand COVID-19 relief package landed in an environment with many control weaknesses.* Auditor General.

Maluleke, T. (2020). *Auditor-General reports significant faults in procurement and contract management processes of COVID-19 relief package.* Auditor General.

Mavuso, S. (2021). Zweli Mkhize allegedly pressured department officials over Digital Vibes tender. https://www.iol.co.za/news/politics/zweli-mkhize-allegedly-pressured-department-officials-over-digital-vibes-tender-d7e9d486-5245-4e53-ae73-45f5230288e9

Merten, M. (2019). State Capture wipes out third of SA's R4.9-trillion GDP—never mind lost trust, confidence, opportunity. *Dailymaverick*, 1 March. https://www.dailymaverick.co.za/article/2019-03-01-state-capture-wipes-out-third-of-sas-r4-9-trillion-gdp-never-mind-lost-trust-confidence-opportunity/

Mnganga-Gcabashe, L. (2018). *Minister of public enterprises update on state-owned companies.* Repeal of Overvaal Resorts Limited Bill, Parliamentary Monitoring Group. https://pmg.org.za/committee-meeting/26819/

Modh, S. (2010). *Introduction to disaster management.* VES Institute of Management Studies and Research, Mumbai.

Mothibi, A. (2021a). *Media statement read by head of the Special Investigating Unit (SIU) Advocate Andy Mothibi during the release of a report of finalised investigations and outcomes of investigations into allegations on the PPE procurement by state institutions—Proclamation R.23 of 2020.* : SIU.

Mothibi, A. (2021b). *Presentation to SCOPA proclamation R23 of 2020 state institution investigations presented by Advocate Andy Mothibi.* SIU.

Nagiah, K. (2012). *The code of conduct of the South African public service compared with international guidelines. Mphil in fraud risk management.* University of Pretoria.

National School of Government. (2020). Minister Senzo Mchunu on compulsory ethics in the public service online course. https://www.gov.za/speeches/minister-senzo-mchunu-ccompulsory-ethics-public-service-online-course-9-sep-2020-0000

National Treasury South Africa. (2020). *COVID-19 instruction note.* National Treasury.

Nkosi, S. (2018). *Management of National Anti-Corruption Hotline (NACH)*. Presentation by Commissioner Nkosi in the Parliament of South Africa, 21 November.

Oduor, M. (2021). Africa's COVID-19 corruption that outweighs pandemic. https://www.africanews.com/2021/05/25/africa-s-COVID-19-corruption-that-outweighs-pandemic/

Office of the Public Service Commission. (1997). *Code of conduct for the public service*. Government Printers.

Oldfield, J. (2020). *Anti-corruption safeguards for economic stimulus packages*. Transparency International Anti-Corruption Helpdesk.

Olken, B. A., & Pande, R. (2012). Corruption in developing countries. *Annual Review of Economics, 4*, 479–509.

Onwujekwe, O., Agwu, P., Orjiakor, C., McKee, M., Hutchinson, E., Mbachu, E., Odii, A., Ogbozor, P., Obi, U., Ichoku, H., & Balabanova, D. (2019). Corruption in anglophone West Africa health systems: A systematic review of its different variants and the factors that sustain them. *Health Policy and Planning, 34*(7), 529–543.

Parliament of South Africa. (2014). *Code of ethical conduct and disclosure of members' interests for assembly and permanent council members*. Parliament.

Parliament of South Africa. (2021). Ethics committee publishes the register of members' interests for 2019. https://www.parliament.gov.za/press-releases/media-statement-ethics-committee-publishes-register-members-interests-2019

Parliamentary Monitoring Group. (2021). Follow up meeting with SIU on investigation into COVID-19 PPE procurement by state institutions. https://pmg.org.za/committee-meeting/33148/

Phakathi, B. (2020). Government mulls setting up special courts to tackle COVID-19 graft. https://www.businesslive.co.za/bd/national/2020-08-27-government-mulls-setting-up-special-courts-to-tackle-COVID-19-graft/

Planting, S. (2021) South Africa's 2021 budget in a box. *Daily Maverick*, 24 February. https://www.dailymaverick.co.za/article/2021-02-24-south-africas-2021-budget-in-a-box/

Public Protector. (2019). *Statement by the Public Protector, Adv. Busisiwe Mkhwebane, during a media briefing held in Pretoria on Friday, July 19, 2019.* http://www.pprotect.org/?q=node/1615

Rakolobe, M. (2019). Politicised public service and corruption in Lesotho. *Strategic Review for Southern Africa, 41*(1).

Ramaphosa, C. (2020a). Statement by President Cyril Ramaphosa on measures to combat COVID-19 epidemic. https://www.gov.za/speeches/statement-president-cyril-ramaphosa-measures-combat-COVID-19-epidemic-15-mar-2020-0000

Ramaphosa, C. (2020b). Additional Coronavirus COVID-19 economic and social relief measures. https://www.gov.za/speeches/president-cyril-ramaphosa-additional-coronavirus-COVID-19-economic-and-social-relief

Reuters. (2021). South Africa probe finds evidence of political pressure, fraud in COVID-19 contracts. 5 February. https://www.reuters.com/article/uk-health-coronavirus-safrica-corruption-idUSKBN2A51GZ

Sabcnews. (2019). Corruption has cost SA close to R1 trillion: Ramaphosa. https://www.sabcnews.com/sabcnews/corruption-has-cost-sa-close-to-r1-trillion-ramaphosa/

Sanews. (2018). PSC receives 472 corruption cases. https://www.sanews.gov.za/south-africa/psc-receives-472-corruption-cases

Schipani, A., Cotterill, J., & Munshi, N. (2020). Africa's COVID-19 corruption: 'Theft doesn't even stop during a pandemic'. https://www.ft.com/content/617187c2-ab0b-4cf9-bdca-0aa246548745

South Africa. (1996). The Constitution of the Republic of South Africa Act of 1996.

South Africa. (1997). Code of conduct for the public service.

South Africa. (1999). Public Finance Management Act 1 of 1999.

South Africa. (2002). The Disaster Management Act 57 of 2002.

Stephen, G. (2021). Bandile Masuku and Zweli Mkhize: Two sides of the same coin? https://www.dailymaverick.co.za/article/2021-05-25-bandile-masuku-and-zweli-mkhize-two-sides-of-the-same-coin/

Transparency International. (2020). *Corruption Perceptions Index 2019.* International Secretariat.

Umraw, A. (2019). Ramaphosa failed to declare R500k Bosasa donation. *Times Live*, 18 April. https://www.timeslive.co.za/politics/2019-04-18-ramaphosa-failed-to-declare-r500k-bosasa-donation-maimane-charges/

United Nations. (2021). Retrieved from Low-income countries have received just 0.2 per cent of all COVID-19 shots given. https://news.un.org/en/story/2021/04/1089392

# 5

# 'Thuma Mina' as a New Ethic of Public Service Accountability in South Africa

## Khali Mofuoa

## Introduction

It is almost half a decade since the former Public Protector, Thuli Madonsela, issued a controversial report famously known as the 'State of Capture' on 14 October 2016. The 'State of Capture' is the report by the Public Protector on an investigation into the allegations of improper and corrupt business relationships and benefits by the state functionaries to the companies linked to the Gupta family in South Africa. Upon receipt of public complaints in connection to the allegations, the Public Protector investigated in terms of section 182(1) (b) of the Constitution of the Republic of South Africa, 1996 read with section 3(1) of the Executive Members Ethics Act and section 8(1) of the Public Protector Act, 1994.

Upon its issuing, it is no secret that the 'State of Capture Report' prompted moral outrage and stunned moral pundits, owing to its exposé of revelations of impunity for fraud and corruption in the South African

K. Mofuoa (✉)
Department of Philosophy, University of Pretoria, Pretoria, South Africa

© The Author(s), under exclusive license to Springer Nature Switzerland AG 2022
K. Ogunyemi et al. (eds.), *Ethics and Accountable Governance in Africa's Public Sector, Volume I*, Palgrave Studies of Public Sector Management in Africa,
https://doi.org/10.1007/978-3-030-95394-2_5

public service. The report exposed a grand scale alleged improper and unethical conduct amongst public service functionaries, including the Office of the Presidency and the Gupta family, a politically connected wealthy Indian-origin family with business interests in South Africa. The Gupta family has been linked to corruption allegations of bribing politicians to advance their business interests during the presidency of Jacob Zuma. Apparently, the Gupta family has been involved in improper relationships and had influenced the removal and appointment of Ministers and Directors of State-Owned Enterprises (Public Protector, 2016, p. 4). Furthermore, this alleged inappropriate relationship between state functionaries and the Gupta family resulted in "possibly corrupt awards of state contracts and benefits to the Gupta family's business empire across the Republic of South Africa" (Public Protector, 2016, p. 4).

The 'State of Capture Report' has created an emotionally and ethically charged environment for South African public service, since its emergence in the public sphere. At the centre of this environment are deafening public outcries for a new ethic of accountability for public service in the Republic of South Africa. Given the report's revelations, the public appeal to ethical accountability in South African public service becomes urgent and warranted. The South African citizenry expects the public service to "become more effective and more efficient, more modern and more intelligent [in its] ways of providing public services" (Ondrová, 2016, p. 395). They expect their public service "also to act with attention to the highest ethical standards" (Bivins, 2006, p. 38). These standards ought "to measure [public service performance] outcomes that are related to the moral and ethical dimension of accountability" (Dicke & Boonyarak, 2005, p. 195). For South Africans, such public expectation is necessary to ensure clean and responsive public service to the citizenry's needs. Most importantly, it is largely expected "to make a decisive break from unchecked abuse of State power and resources that was virtually institutionalised during the apartheid era" (Public Protector, 2016, p. 3).

President Cyril Ramaphosa ascended to the two most important presidencies in South African body-politic with high public optimism and euphoria, amid the public outcries resulting from the shocking revelations of the 'State of Capture' impropriety. First, in December 2017, he became president of the ruling party, African National Congress (ANC).

Second, in 2018, he became the fifth democratically elected president of the Republic of South Africa. In both presidencies, he succeeded former President Jacob Zuma who was implicated in the 'State of Capture' malfeasance. People expected Ramaphosa's presidencies to bring about a new lease of life for a public service probity in which accountability to the citizenry would be rekindled. Generally, the public perception within South African citizenry is that "people are concerned about the integrity and standards of public administrators' behaviour, their ethical and professional competence in decision-making processes, asking for stronger responsiveness to the interests of public service users" (Ondrová, 2016, p. 396). They simply wanted change in the management, administration, and governance of public affairs by their public service.

President Ramaphosa did not disappoint South Africans as Thuma Mina became the punchline or tagline of his sixth administration and presidency. The term or concept of Thuma Mina is an action-inspired philosophical and ideological break with South Africa's state of capture past and a vehicle for an ethically revitalised South Africa in the service of the citizenry through the Batho Pele—People First service slogan 'We Belong, We Care, We Service'. It is also seen as a transformative idea of positioning South Africa in the new path of socio-economic and political development that prioritises ethics and accountable governance in the public service. It is further understood as a rallying ideal or slogan for ethical transformation of South Africa to galvanise South Africans to join hands in a common national crusade for a new public sense of optimism for a morally inspired corruption-free future.

As a new dawn action-inspired message, Thuma Mina became a way for President Ramaphosa to summon the spirit of the country's struggle history to tackle the problems of today, particularly the fixing of the damage of 'State of Capture'– a period termed the 'lost decade' under the presidency of Jacob Zuma. Thus, in all its ramifications, Thuma Mina promised an ethically inspired transformative change to South Africans on how the public service goes about its business to the citizenry. In essence, as much as Thuma Mina is a South African call for moral responsibility to clean public service, the reader should interpret it as a continental rallying cry for ethics and accountable governance in Africa's public sector and break with the cancerous and rampant proportions of corruption in Africa (Jones, 2021; Imiera, 2020, pp. 70–89; Duri, 2020, pp. 1–29; Mbaku, 2010; Hope, 2000, pp. 17–39; Olivier de Sardan, 1999, pp. 25–52). Lamenting about the state of corruption engulfing the African continent, Duri (2020, p. 1) remarks,

> Across sub-Saharan Africa, many countries are making considerable prog-ress towards the vision of a democratic, prosperous, and peaceful continent outlined in the African Union's Agenda 2063. However, gains are threat-ened by high levels of corruption.

The chapter presents Thuma Mina as a new ethic of accountability for the South African public service, to bring about much-needed ethical and accountable governance in South Africa in the aftermath of 'State of Capture' that eroded public service probity. In essence, the South African citizenry has embraced Thuma Mina as a renewed focus on ethical stan-dards in response to the widespread evidence of declining public confi-dence and trust in the South African public service. The chapter has six sections, of which "Introduction" section introduces it. "Thuma Mina: Its Genesis, Roots, and Popularity" section explores Thuma Mina's gene-sis, roots, and popularity. "Thuma Mina: Taking Stock of Its Spirit, Ethics, and Ethos" section outlines the spirit, ethos, and ethics of Thuma Mina. "Thuma Mina: Its Salient Ethical Traits for South African Public Service Leaders" section discusses the salient ethical traits or qualities that Thuma Mina's infuses in the context of public service leadership. "Thuma Mina: Its Initial Critical Performance Impact Assessment" section makes a brief performance assessment of Thuma Mina as a new South African public service ethic after the state capture era. "Conclusion" section con-cludes the chapter.

## Thuma Mina: Its Genesis, Roots, and Popularity

With its colonial-apartheid roots, South African public service is always prone or susceptible to evils of abuse of State power as mirrored by the 'State of Capture.' Perhaps, the year 2016 went down in history as one of the most revealing years in terms of moral brokenness of the public service in post-apartheid and democratic South Africa. It witnessed the release of an ethically scandalous 'State of Capture' report by the Office of Public Protector South Africa, exposing systemic political fraud and corruption in public service. The report is the latest mega moral meltdown in a string of South African public service scandals in recent years, which have undermined ethics and accountable governance in South Africa's public sector.

Amid the morally devastating revelations of the 'State of Capture' to the South African public psyche, Mr Cyril Ramaphosa in 2017 ascended to the presidency of the ruling party, the African National Congress (ANC) and, in 2018, that of the Republic of South Africa. His ascension to these politically powerful presidencies was hailed as a 'New Dawn' since the nation seemed to have finally woken to the reality of the loss of its post-apartheid internationally acclaimed moral righteousness, innocence, and reputation. President Ramaphosa was strategic enough to go with the public mood and skilfully attached his political tactics to the national sense of loss by publicly declaring: "Yes, South Africa, Thuma Mina." He famously said, "Yes, Thuma Mina," for the first time, upon taking the reins of the fifth administration from his predecessor, President Jacob Zuma. After that, Thuma Mina has dominated President Ramaphosa's sixth administration and presidency era with a new public sense of optimism for a morally inspired South African future free from the shackles of corruption.

The genesis of Thuma Mina and its use by President Ramaphosa are well documented in Mashau and Kgatle (2021), Kloppers (2020), Barnard-Naudé (2020), Beckmann (2019), Göranzon (2019), and Maluleke (2018). Thuma Mina is a common expression in Southern African societies with varying indigenous language expressions yet bearing similar meanings. For instance, in Southern Africa Bantu languages, the word would be 'Roma Nna' in Sotho languages of the Basotho, Bapeli, and Batswana; and 'Thuma Mina' in Nguni languages of Zulus, Xhosas, Ndebeles, and Swazis (Mashau & Kgatle, 2021). The phrase 'Thuma Mina' or 'Roma Nna' means 'send me' (Göranzon, 2019, p. 175), which implies taking a morally inspired action by everyone for the service of others irrespective of the context, be in the community or public service.

It is a famous and widespread expression in Southern Africa's Bantu languages in various contexts making a clarion call for moral responsibility and accountability.

First, Thuma Mina's popularity is found in South African churches as favourite praise and worship song (Göranzon, 2019, p. 19). This is because Thuma Mina has its scriptural roots in Isaiah 6:8 (Maluleke, 2018). This biblical heritage has made it the most famous hymn of church music praise and worship songs, igniting the spirit and practice of service to others in traditional governance discourses of communities (Nzimakwe, 2014; Meylahn & Musiyambiri, 2017). The most favourite lyrics or stanzas of 'Here am I Lord send me' hymn aka Thuma Mina, read like: *Here am I Lord send me; Here am I Lord send me; I will serve You faithfully; Here am I Lord send me* (Musixmatch, n.d.). The hymn's lyrics popularity is associated mainly with the importance of Isaiah in the Bible. The Prophet Isaiah is best known for predicting the coming or the 'sending' of Jesus Christ by God to salvage humanity. Thus, Thuma Mina carries and bears a biblical ministerial message for action-inspired calling in the service to others in the context of delivery of public services to the citizenry. In a sense, Thuma Mina underscores the influence of biblical scriptures in public governance.

Second, Thuma Mina's popularity also has roots in the most-loved Afro-jazz genre of the South African music industry promoted by the likes of the late legend Hugh Masekela. Thus, Thuma Mina is best referred to as the late Masekela's anthemic song of all time (Thamm, 2018). It is a song about solidarity, compassion, and renewal (Thamm, 2018). It was composed by Hugh Masekela, Sello Twala, and gospel star, Peter Mokoena (Thamm, 2018). It was recorded in Johannesburg and released through Sony and Columbia labels in 2002, eight years after the dawn of democracy in South Africa (Maluleke, 2018). Since its release, Thuma Mina connected with the public mood, as it kept its feet on the ground at home while igniting a sense of general jubilation for action to confront the pressing societal challenges of South Africa. Indeed, Thuma Mina's message for action vibrated across the entire spectrum of South Africa, challenging everyone to participate in addressing societal problems such as HIV/Aids, violence, poverty, and gender-based violence, not just with words but also with deeds.

Third, Thuma Mina's popularity has now recently found its new home in the body politic of South Africa on two critical fronts. On 16 February 2018 when President Ramaphosa "rose in Parliament to deliver his inaugural State of the Nation Address, invoking the lyrics of Thuma Mina song by struggle and music icon Hugh Masekela" (Lediga, 2018). On 25 May 2018, the new President gave his inauguration speech, declaring, "Having taken the oath of office, I am saying yes South Africa, Thuma Mina" (Nagel, 2020). Upon making Thuma Mina's public declaration, two critical things happened: Ramaphosa formally "became the Thuma Mina president" (Nagel, 2020) and he gave rise to the Thuma Mina movement in South Africa.

Thuma Mina became President Ramaphosa's socio-political master effort "to galvanize all South Africans to action to reverse the negative effects of the excesses of the Zuma presidency" (Lediga, 2018). In the South Africa of the former President Zuma era, Maluleka in Nagel (2020) reckons that "people no longer wanted to say, 'send me' unless there was something in it for them." Maluleke in Nagel (2020) argues that this behaviour is indicated by the revelations of the 'State of Capture' in which alleged private interests significantly influenced the state's decision-making processes to their advantage at the expense of public interests, which is at the heart of the delivery of public services to the citizenry. Lediga (2018) agrees that, as witnessed by the revelations of the 'State of Capture', "by the time [President] Ramaphosa invoked Thuma Mina, South Africa had experienced [almost a decade] of destructive and devastating rule by [former President] Zuma." Hence, Lediga (2018) submits, "President Ramaphosa's new dawn message had to invoke Thuma Mina to join hands in a common national crusade to fix the [morally broken South Africa in the post-Apartheid era]."

# Thuma Mina: Taking Stock of Its Spirit, Ethics, and Ethos

Since President Ramaphosa's ground-breaking State of the Nation Address (SONA) speech on 16 February 2018, "Thuma Mina instantaneously forced its way into the social and political lexicon of the rainbow nation" (Lediga, 2018). President's Thuma Mina speech seemed to have suddenly, in a socially, morally, and politically profound way, "struck the right chord with the nation [as] South Africans of all hues were ready to serve" (Lediga, 2018). The speech's reception by South Africans was "captivating as its delivery met rousing applause and a standing ovation from people of all walks of life" (Ka-Ndyalvan, 2018).

It was like the spirit of Thuma Mina has filled entire South Africa once more, spurring all South Africans into action to pursue what Lediga (2018) describes as "a noble, nation-building programme of Thuma Mina to tackle state capture graft and other socio-political issues in South Africa." Agreeing with the spirit of Thuma Mina sentiments expressed in Lediga (2018), Ka-Ndyalvan (2018) sees Thuma Mina as "a spirit of self-conviction that brought colonial apartheid to its knees [in South Africa]." Some political commentators see Thuma Mina as "a way to summon the spirit of [South Africa's] struggle history to tackle the problems of today [like] tackling state capture at state-owned entities" (Mail & Guardian, 2019). The ruling party, African National Congress (ANC) sees Thuma Mina as "embracing the spirit of selflessness and restoration of people's conscience to serve others" (ANC, 2019). Mashau and Kgatle (2021, p. 1) conclude that Thuma Mina is "the spirit of volunteerism, servanthood and sacrifice to bring about lasting solutions to challenges of decay [i.e., moral, social, economic, etc.] that South Africa faces." Maluleke (2018) in Nagel (2020) agrees with Mashau and Kgatle (2021) that the spirit of Thuma Mina is mirrored in Masekela's life as "one of the most astute interpreters of the social issues of his times." Here, Maluleke (2018) in Nagel (2020) argues, "the spirit of Thuma Mina is reflected in Masekela's music as a direct result of his sensitivity and alertness to social issues."

Beyond arousing the spirit of Thuma Mina, "Ramaphosa's inaugural SONA in February 2018 ignited the ethos of Thuma Mina" (Oxford, 2018). In this regard, Oxford (2018) contends that Thuma Mina "has become the South African call to action that all citizens work together to create a better country." With Thuma Mina, Oxford (2018) argues, "Ramaphosa's vision was simple—everyone has a role to play in changing the future of an embattled [South Africa]." In agreement, Mashau and Kgatle (2021, p. 6) state that Thuma Mina is an "[ethic] even for a South African style of governance [in the public service]." Here, ethic means a set of moral principle affirming Thuma Mina, that is, service to others, and ethos refers to the attitudes and aspirations manifested in Thuma Mina. Thus, the ethos of Thuma Mina has been used in the public service ethics as a call for South Africans to accept the public duty to serve the beleaguered nation selflessly. In this regard, the ethos of Thuma Mina has subsequently been used in various public service campaigns and programmes by the government. This has been done to ensure that Thuma Mina remains and thrives in the public consciousness to spur them to action against cancerous malfeasance of fraud and corruption in the public service.

Finally, beyond igniting the ethos of Thuma Mina, President Ramaphosa's inaugural SONA in February 2018 rekindled the ethics of Thuma Mina (Reddy, 2019). For Reddy (2019), Thuma Mina calls for a new ethics of responsibility in the public service whose objective is to place leadership or management at the centre of accountability and responsibility, focusing on ethical outcomes. It is also a call for promoting ethical standards within the public service and a corporate culture that embraces them. In broad terms, in the words of President Ramaphosa, it is a call to "forge a compact for an efficient, capable, and ethical state, a state that is free from corruption, for elected officials and publics who faithfully serve no other cause than that of the public" (Shange, 2019). Thus, the ethics of Thuma Mina in the public service is about how the leadership behaves and fulfils their responsibilities that drive the ethical behaviour of public servants and the ethical outcomes they deliver. In turn, the resulting ethical behaviours and outcomes measure the effectiveness of the tone from the leadership at the top.

# Thuma Mina: Its Salient Ethical Traits for South African Public Service Leaders

In his State of the Nation Address (SONA) on 16 February 2018, President Ramaphosa famously quoted the Thuma Mina song by the late Hugh Masekela as follows:

> *I wanna be there when the people start to turn it around.*
> *When they triumph over poverty.*
> *I wanna be there when the people win the battle against AIDS.*
> *I wanna lend a hand.*
> *I wanna be there for the alcoholic.*
> *I wanna be there for the victims of violence and abuse.*
> *I wanna lend a hand.*
> *Send me (Thuma Mina)*
> Source: Mashau and Kgatle (2021, p. 4)

When President Ramaphosa read out Thuma Mina lyrics in his SONA speech, nobody knew that "Thuma Mina [would become] a metaphor of hope and renewal for the ANC and [South African] society in general" (Hunter, 2020). Most profoundly, nobody knew that Thuma Mina would come "to embody the spirit of [Ramaphosa's] presidency" (Hunter, 2020). Irrespective of which angle one looks at it, Thuma Mina's speech by President Ramaphosa "injected [South Africa] with a level of [unparallel hope and] optimism unknown over a decade [that ringfenced his rise to the presidency]" (Hunter, 2020). According to Thamm (2018), President Ramaphosa's speech marked the start of the Thuma Mina era. The era that inspires South Africans as a rainbow nation to serve each other beyond racial and tribal lines (Shambala, 2020). The era that also encourages "the spirit of volunteerism—not just volunteering [one's] services for a noble task of serving South Africa, [but] also making efforts to inspire South Africans to do the same" (Mashau & Kgatle, 2021, p. 4). The president's speech was publicly acknowledged as "a call for South Africans to find new inspiration and hope in a common humanity, ubuntu duty and service" (Thamm, 2018).

The newly ushered Thuma Mina era received augmented status "in the address by former Minister of Public Service and Administration, Ayanda Dlodlo at the launch of the 2018 public service month" (Polity, 2018). The theme of the launch was "Thuma Mina—Taking Public Service to the people: Batho Pele—People First" (Polity, 2018). Within the context of South African public service, former Minister Ayanda Dlodlo described Thuma Mina as a clarion call to public servants "to comply to the standards of the Batho Pele Principles of accountability, quality of service and commitment [to the service of others]" (Polity, 2018). She expressly stated that Thuma Mina is a blood life of the Batho Pele principles, "with an enduring vision to instill and rebuild good ethics [in the South African public service's duty to serve others] with efficiency, diligence, and integrity" (Polity, 2018). She concluded her address by emphatically stating that, in the Thuma Mina's duty to serve others, "[South Africa] needs a public service that is developmental, caring, and progressive [and] that is professional, responsive, capable, and responsible" (Polity, 2018).

At the heart of Thuma Mina's duty to serve others are the salient ethical qualities of "desire to lead, drive, self-confidence, honesty (and integrity), cognitive ability, and industry knowledge" (Kirkpatrick & Locke, 1991, pp. 48–60). Each of the ethical qualities' characteristic of Thuma Mina is discussed below. One of the salient qualities of the Thuma Mina is "the desire to lead others into action 'but not to seek power as an end in itself'" (Kirkpatrick & Locke, 1991, p. 48). Studies show that Thuma Mina leaders who have a strong desire to lead are motivated to use their socialised power to influence others to pursue a particular course of action in the service of others (Kirkpatrick & Locke, 1991, p. 52). In addition, they are willing to assume responsibility for their actions and that of others (Kirkpatrick & Locke, 1991, p. 52). Thuma Mina leaders use socialised power to achieve desired goals cooperatively with others. Kirkpatrick and Locke (1991, p. 53) state that Thuma Mina leaders' use of their socialised power is expressed in their ability to develop networks and coalitions, gain cooperation from others, constructively resolve conflicts, and use role modelling to influence others. Kirkpatrick and Locke (1991, p. 58) opine "without the desire to lead, individuals are not motivated to persuade others to work toward a common goal; such an individual would avoid or be indifferent to leadership task [in the service of others]."

One of the salient qualities of Thuma Mina is the drive to motivate others into action. In broad terms, drive as a quality refers to "a constellation of traits and motives reflecting a high effort level" (Kirkpatrick & Locke, 1991, p. 48). Kirkpatrick and Locke (1991, p. 48) note that the aspects of the drive as a quality "includes achievement, motivation, ambition, energy, tenacity, and initiative." The drive for achievement is an essential motive for Thuma Mina leaders as "High achievers obtain satisfaction from completing challenging tasks, attaining standards of excellence, and developing better ways of doing thing" (Kirkpatrick & Locke, 1991, p. 49). With the drive to achieve change or transformation in the service of others, the Thuma Mina leaders are very ambitious to set challenging goals for themselves. However, the ambition to set challenging for oneself is scarce quality in the public service as few leaders embody it. The Thuma Mina leaders also have the energy and tenacity to complete assigned tasks for the benefit of others. Incidentally, Kirkpatrick and Locke (1991, p. 58) state that "without the drive, it is unlikely that a [leader] would be able to gain the expertise required to lead [others to complete agreed tasks] effectively, let alone implement and work toward [achieving] long-term goals in the service of others."

Self-confidence, which is associated with emotional stability, is one of the striking qualities of Thuma Mina. According to Kirkpatrick and Locke (1991, p. 54), "self-confidence plays an important role in decision-making and in gaining confidence and trust of others [towards completion of a set task in the service of others]." Kirkpatrick and Locke (1991, p. 58) argue, "self-confidence is needed to withstand setbacks, persevere through hard times, and lead others in new directions. Confidence gives effective leaders the ability to make hard decisions and to stand by them." With radiating self-confidence, a Thuma Mina leader is likely to be "assertive and decisive [in the service of others], which gains others' confidence in the decision" (Kirkpatrick & Locke, 1991, p. 54). By projecting self-confidence in the service of others, a Thuma Mina leader stimulates self-confidence in others to work cooperatively to ensure the completion of the set goal or task. Kirkpatrick and Locke (1991, p. 54) stipulate the importance of Thuma Mina's self-confidence in decision-making thus, "Even when the decision turns out to be a poor one, the self-confident [Thuma Mina] leader admits the mistake and uses it as a learning opportunity, often building trust in the process."

Honesty and integrity are some of the conspicuous qualities of Thuma Mina, as people always want to assure themselves that they are served by someone worthy of their trust. Kirkpatrick and Locke (1991, p. 53) point out that "Integrity is the correspondence between word and deed [while] honesty refers to being truthful or non-deceitful." The importance of honesty and integrity as Thuma Mina traits is that they "form the foundation of a trusting relationship between [Thuma Mina leader and the people they serve]" (Kirkpatrick & Locke, 1991, p. 53). In essence, honesty and integrity "form the foundation on which the [Thuma Mina] leader gains trust and confidence [of people she serves]" (Kirkpatrick & Locke, 1991, p. 53). It follows, therefore, that without the qualities of honesty and integrity, the Thuma Mina leader would not receive trusting support from others. Thus, being truthful, ethical, and principled are at the heart of honesty and integrity as salient qualities of Thuma Mina. This is so because people generally want to be fully confident in the integrity of someone who serves them.

Emotional stability, which is associated with self-confidence, is one of the prominent qualities of Thuma Mina. Kirkpatrick and Locke (1991, p. 55) indicate that, in most cases, "leaders are more likely to 'derail' if they lack emotional stability and composure." According to Kirkpatrick and Locke (1991, p. 55), "leaders who derail are less able to handle pressure and more prone to moodiness, angry outbursts, and inconsistent behaviour, which undermines their interpersonal relationships with others." In contrast, Thuma Mina leaders are often calm, confident, and non-impulsive as they have exceptional emotional stability and composure. The quality of emotional stability enables Thuma Mina leaders to deal with stressful and conflict-ridden situations. Stressful and conflict-ridden situations provide opportunities for Thuma Mina leaders to use their exceptional emotional stability trait to influence the outcomes of their public engagements in the service of others. By demonstrating emotional stability and composure in stressful and conflict-ridden situations, Thuma Mina "leaders inspire those around them to stay calm and act intelligently [in the service of others]" (Kirkpatrick & Locke, 1991, p. 55).

One of the noticeable qualities of Thuma Mina is cognitive ability. Gottfredson (1997, p. 13) defines cognitive ability as a "mental capacity that involves the ability to reason, solve problems, think abstractly, comprehend complex ideas, learn quickly and learn from experience." In agreement with Gottfredson's definition of cognitive ability, Kirkpatrick and Locke (1991, p. 58) argue, "at least a moderate degree of cognitive ability is needed for leaders to accurately analyse situations and make effective decisions [in the service of others]." Thuma Mina leaders with cognitive ability as a trait are able, in the service of others, "to make well-informed decisions and to understand the implications of those decisions" (Kirkpatrick & Locke, 1991, p. 56).

Finally, knowledge of the business of being in the service of others is one of the exceptional qualities of Thuma Mina. Barreira (2004) contends that, in any given business-like context, "one cannot downplay the influence of business knowledge in achieving set goals or tasks." In agreeing with Barreira's sentiments, Kirkpatrick and Locke (1991, p. 58) state, "knowledge of the business is needed to develop suitable strategic visions and business plans [to achieve a set goal or task]." In fact, according to Achrnews (2017) "a lack of business knowledge often leads to failure." By mastering business knowledge of serving others, Thuma Mina leaders can be on their way to running an impactful business in the service of others with a firm understanding of their decision-making processes to positively impact the lives of others.

## Thuma Mina: Its Initial Critical Performance Impact Assessment

The significance of President Ramaphosa's rallying the late Hugh Masekela's song 'Thuma Mina'—'Send Me' as a call for public service accountability and responsibility cannot be overstressed. Thuma Mina touched people's hearts and energised many South Africans into action to personally contribute more towards bettering the country. Ansell (2019) states that Thuma Mina also became "a leitmotif for the Ramaphosa presidency." Ansell (2019) contends that "it was no surprise that during inauguration speech in 2018 [Ramaphosa] famously invoked Thuma Mina." In Ansell's view, "even before he became president, [Ramaphosa] relished the South African jazz that spoke for and of the country's liberation struggle [ethos of self-sacrifice, servitude, and individual responsibility]" (Ansell, 2019).

Since starting the Thuma Mina movement, President Ramaphosa "has been rolling up his sleeves to win over the hearts of South Africans [to urge them to embrace the business of being in the service of others in the true Thuma Mina ethos]" (Mjo, 2018). Here are the most remarkable Thuma Mina moments of President Ramaphosa since his presidencies of the ANC and the country. The first Thuma Mina moment relates to promoting healthy living among South Africans through presidential lifestyle walks. One cannot overstress the benefits of a healthy nation from Thuma Mina perspective amid the Covid-19 pandemic. Therefore, it is not surprising that "promoting healthy living is one of the pillars of the [President Ramaphosa's Thuma Mina presidency]." Through Thuma Mina's presidential lifestyle walks, President Ramaphosa participated in several walks throughout the country. These included the Old Mutual Soweto Marathon, Gandhi Walk, Durban Walk, SOWETO Walk, and Cape Town Walk, to mention a few. Mjo (2018) notes that the Thuma Mina presidential lifestyle walks actually "left many [South Africans] on social media extremely impressed [for encouraging people to take responsibly for their health]."

The second Thuma Mina moment relates to the tackling of youth unemployment in South Africa. Graham et al. (2021) state that "youth unemployment is one of South Africa's most intractable challenges, made worse by the Covid-19 pandemic." Early days in his Thuma Mina presidency, President Ramaphosa made tackling youth unemployment his priority. Mjo (2018) notes, "he partnered with the private sector, labour, and civil society to launch the Youth Employment Service (YES) initiative." In the spirit of Thuma Mina, the YES initiative encourages corporates to address youth unemployment and upskilling through job creation, and it is continuing to succeed in this regard. At the launch of YES initiative, President Ramaphosa described the initiative as "set to change the lives of many young people [by ensuring that they] have the skills that [the South African] economy needs" (Khoza, 2018).

Through Thuma Mina presidential drive, President Ramaphosa has also "hosted a jobs summit [for] various stakeholders from business, government, and labour to find solutions to the plight of [youth] unemployment" (Mjo, 2018). Mjo (2018) indicates, "One of the summit outcomes was a target of 275,000 jobs a year." In addition, in the spirit of Thuma Mina, the Presidential Youth Employment Intervention (PYEI), in partnership with business, government, and labour, has created the SA Youth network for all young people to access learning opportunities for free that support (1) "a capable and developmental state that adhere[s] to Batho Pele principles, by putting People First [in the delivery of public services]" (Polity, 2018) and that support (2) "small and medium enterprises and garner more investments in the economy [to address] the most pressing socio-economic challenges in the country, particularly poverty and unemployment among the youth" (Khoza, 2018).

The third Thuma Mina moment relates to the presidential drive of encouraging investment in the South African economy by national and international investors. One of the critical priorities of the Thuma Mina presidency of Cyril Ramaphosa is "to revive the South African economy in the post-Zuma era" (Mjo, 2018). In the early days of his Thuma Mina presidency, President Ramaphosa "announced plans to attract $100-billion in investments over five years" (Mjo, 2018). In the true spirit of Thuma Mina, Mjo (2018) mentions, "[President Ramaphosa] passed the halfway mark of [$100-billion] target within six months of launching the investment drive." Two crucial initiatives made this possible: first, President Ramaphosa "set up a special task team, which travelled around the world in search for investments" (Mjo, 2018; Kgosana, 2018). Second, President Ramaphosa "hosted an investment summit, where local and foreign companies made pledges worth $20b to the South African economy" (Mjo, 2018; Kgosana, 2018). For example, Kgosana (2018) notes, "Thuma Mina encouraged Anglo American to invest R71.5 bn into the South African economy over five years through extending its operations." In addition, the Thuma Mina Presidential Investment "drive attracted investments from China, United Aran Emirates, the United Kingdom and Saudi Arabia" (Mjo, 2018). The summit was attended by "at least 1000 delegates, comprising local and international business leaders, government officials, and civil society" (Kgosana, 2018).

The fourth Thuma Mina moment relates to tackling state capture at the South African state-owned entities or enterprises (SOEs) and public institutions. In his SONA 2019 speech, President Ramaphosa underlined the need "to deal with the effects of the state capture on vital public institutions, including law enforcement agencies whose integrity and ability to fulfil their mandate had been eroded in recent years" (Timeslive, 2019). Therefore, it is not surprising that tackling state capture became a central priority in the Thuma Mina presidency of Cyril Ramaphosa. He expressly stated in his SONA 2019 speech, "[his administration] has no choice but to step up the fight against corruption and state capture" (Timeslive, 2019).

In the drive to fix the South African SOEs and public institutions, President Ramaphosa took ground-breaking Thuma Mina actions: First, he announced a new Board of Directors for Eskom, which he instructed to remove all executives facing allegations of serious corruption. Second, he appointed commissions of inquiry into tax administration and into the National Prosecuting Authority (NPA), which led to the dismissal of top officials. Third, he established a special unit within the NPA to specialise in corruption-related crimes (Alence & Pitcher, 2019). Omarjee (2021) is of the view that these Thuma Mina actions were expressly indicative of President Ramaphosa Administration's promise that "if needed, [action] will be [taken] against those who are implicated in the state capture of SOEs [and public institutions as the case may be]." Through these Thuma Mina actions, President Ramaphosa made good on his promise of taking the fight against corruption to clean up the public service.

The fifth and final Thuma Mina moment relates to rebuilding the public service to support an efficient, capable, and ethical state "in improving the lacking government's service delivery and accountability" (Beckmann, 2019). Under the 2018 Public Service Month themed 'Thuma Mina,' South African public servants pledged to take Public Service to the people (SAnews, 2018). Through the Batho Pele service slogan 'We Belong, We Care, We Service' inspired by Thuma Mina, South African public servants further pledged to (1) put people first in delivery of public services and (2) create a conducive working environment, which instils a sense of belonging to all (SAnews, 2018). The Thuma Mina call to rebuild the public service was also embraced by the ANC Caucus in the South

African parliament. In the spirit of Thuma Mina, Gerber (2019) states that "ANC chief whip want[ed] compulsory ethics training for all MPs during the sixth Parliament's term of Ramaphosa's Presidency." The ANC parliamentary caucus believes that "[the] focus on raising the standards of ethical conduct from public representatives will go a long way in efforts to fight against corruption and state capture" (Gerber, 2019).

Inspired by Thuma Mina's presidential call to rebuild the public service, "in the sixth Parliament, the ANC parliamentary caucus [has] dedicated itself to primarily serve the people of South Africa" (Gerber, 2019). In this regard, the ANC parliamentary caucus has pledged (1) to instil strict discipline in the ANC caucus to ensure that members of the parliament (MPs) attend committee meetings and sittings; (2) partner with civil society organisations to address the challenges faced by communities; (3) follow up on the challenges raised by communities, working together with local government, and (4) to strengthen oversight over government, and for restructuring of SOEs to ensure good returns on public funds invested in them (Gerber, 2019).

Notwithstanding the above-enumerated instructive and positive Thuma Mina moments, the presidencies of Ramaphosa continue to be challenged by the cancer of corruption in the public service and the ranks of the ANC. The widespread corruption by officials in the public service threatens to derail the wheels of Thuma Mina as poor ethics and corruption continue to find their way into the DNA of the public service and the ranks of the ruling party. Here, Booysen (2021) doubts the efficacy of the ruling party's Thuma Mina efforts to 'self-correct' and to fight corruption because "as far as 1999 the [ANC] acknowledged the existence of corruption in its ranks [and] since then corruption has become endemic." Correspondingly, the public service has seen a rise in corrupt activities by officials as the ruling party government admits that "corruption continue to taint SA's public service" (Felix, 2021). However, Booysen (2021) still believes that President "Ramaphosa's rise to power [on the Thuma Mina ticket], from when he became ANC president in December 2017, and the country's president in February 2018, offered South Africans hope that he would clean up the corruption [in the public service]."

Through the backdrop of Thuma Mina ticket, Booysen (2021) argues that "indeed, [President Ramaphosa has] made good on the promise to clean up the corruption." Here, President Ramaphosa swiftly established "the new corruption-bursting unit within the office of the National Directorate of Public Prosecutions (NDPP)" (Etheridge, 2019), moving observers to remark, "[Is] Thuma Mina a new beginning for South Africa?" (Martin, 2018). However, cynicism about and around Thuma Mina still exists with pundits contending that it remains to be seen how far the fight against corruption would go as President Ramaphosa's administration "pursues to build ethical ANC, ethical state, and ethical public service that act against corruption under the Thuma Mina project" (Njilo, 2021). Pundits also say that it remains to be seen how far Thuma Mina ticket can help President Ramaphosa's administration (1) to effectively make "all public servants to become agents of change" (Polity, 2018) and (2) to successfully instil a new South African Public Service work ethic "to do things correctly, to do them completely and to do them timeously" (Polity, 2018).

# Conclusion

President Ramaphosa's Thuma Mina "presents an alternative, aspirational vision for South Africa that is focussed on spurring [active citizenry for good governance and public good]" (Markle & Cilliers, 2020). Mashau and Kgatle (2021, p. 6) states that, "the Thuma Mina ethos is more than a song and a biblical phrase; it is viable and practical even for a South African style of governance [in public affairs]." Similarly, Azania (2020) sees Thuma Mina as "much bigger than an electioneering slogan [but] a commitment to righting the wrongs, to correcting injustices and to healing the wounds [of South African] democratic dispensation." Conclusively, in the eyes of South Africans, Thuma Mina is a new ethic of public service accountability and responsibility in South Africa with the promise of "dislodging the corrupt networks of 'state capture' entrenched under former President Jacob Zuma" (Alence & Pitcher, 2019, p. 5). It is the driver of President Ramaphosa's 'new dawn' to bring about a new lease of life for public service probity to remove "the stain of corruption [that] attached itself to [former President Jacob] Zuma for much of the past two decades" (Martin, 2018). It is a new ethic of accountability and responsibility for the South African public service to bring about much-needed ethical and accountable governance in South Africa after 'state capture,' which eroded public service probity. That said, however, it remains to be seen if Thuma Mina would persist as "a driver to mobilise South Africans to embrace the spirit of volunteerism, servanthood and sacrifice to bring about lasting solutions to challenges of decay that South Africa faces" (Mashau & Kgatle, 2021, p. 1). Most urgent, it remains to be seen if Thuma Mina would slow the wheels of corruption in the South African public service and help government to improve its handle of anti-corruption fight effectively to stamp out corruption and create corruption-free South Africa. Indeed, South Africa's getting to Thuma Mina not just in word but also in deed, and to take accountability for corruption can be exemplary to the rest of the African continent.

# References

Achrnews. (2017). A lack of business knowledge often leads to failure. *ACHR News*. Retrieved June 14, 2021, from https://www.achrnews.com/articles/135759-a-lack-of-business-knowledge-often-leads-to-failure

African National Congress. (2019). ANC roll-out a nationwide Thuma Mina programme. *ANC1912*. Retrieved June 2, 2021, from https://anc1912.org.za/updates/anc-roll-out-nation-wide-thuma-mina-programme

Alence, R., & Pitcher, A. (2019). Resisting state capture in South Africa. *Journal of Democracy, 30*(4), 5–19.

Ansell, G. (2019). Jonas Gwangwa's music and life embody the resistance against apartheid. *The Conversation*. Retrieved June 16, 2021, from https://theconversation.com/jonas-gwangwas-music-and-life-embody-the-resistance-against-apartheid-118792

Azania, M. W. (2020). *Corridors of dearth: Struggling to exist in historically white institutions*. Blackbird Books.

Barnard-Naudé, J. (2020). We must be able to get used to the real. *Philosophy & Rhetoric, 53*(3), 217–224. https://doi.org/10.5325/philrhet.53.3.0217

Barreira, J. C. D. (2004). *The influence of business knowledge and work experience, as antecedents to entrepreneurial success*. Philosophiae Doctor thesis, Faculty of Economic and Management Sciences, University of Pretoria.

Beckmann, J. (2019). Thuma Mina and education: Volunteerism, possibilities, and challenges. *South African Journal of Education, 39*(1), 1–8.

Bivins, T. (2006). Responsibility and accountability. In K. Fitzpatrick & C. Bronstein (Eds.), *Ethics public relations: Responsible advocacy*. SAGE Publications, Inc.

Booysen, S. (2021). Precarious power tilts towards Ramaphosa in battle inside South Africa's governing party. *The Conversation*. Retrieved June 16, 2021, from https://theconversation.com/precarious-power-tilts-towards-ramaphosa-in-battle-inside-south-africas-governing-party-158251

Dicke, L. A., & Boonyarak, P. (2005). Ensuring accountability in human services: Dilemma of measuring moral and ethical performance. In H. G. Frederickson & R. K. Ghere (Eds.), *Ethics in public management*. M.E. Sharpe, Inc.

Duri, J. (2020). Sub-Saharan Africa: Overview of corruption and anti-corruption. *U4 Helpdesk Answer*. U4 Anti-Corruption Resource Centre, Chr. Michelson Institute.

Etheridge, J. (2019). South Africans offer 'Thuma Mina' for Ramaphosa's new corruption bursting unit. *News24*. Retrieved June 26, 2021, from https://www.news24.com/news24/southafrica/news/south-africans-offer-thuma-mina-for-ramaphosas-new-corruption-busting-unit-20190208

Felix, J. (2021). Laziness, incompetence and corruption continue to taint SA's public service – Senzo Mchunu. *News24*. Retrieved June 26, 2021, from https://www.news24.com/news24/southafrica/news/laziness-incompetence-and-corruption-continue-to-taint-sas-public-service-senzo-mchunu-20210603

Gerber, J. (2019). ANC chief whip wants compulsory ethics training for all MPs. *News24*. Retrieved June 21, 2021, from https://www.news24.com/news24/southafrica/news/anc-chief-whip-wants-compulsory-ethics-training-for-all-mps-20190909

Göranzon, A. (2019). Thuma mina! Who sends whom? How South Africa as a Rainbow Nation has been perceived in the Church of Sweden. *Alternation, 26*(1), 174–193. https://doi.org/10.29086/2519-5476/2019/v26n1a8

Gottfredson, L. S. (1997). Why g matters: The complexity of everyday life. *Intelligence, 24*(1), 79–132.

Graham, L., De Lannoy, A., & Patel, L. (2021). South Africa's efforts to tackle joblessness can be more effective: Here's how. *Biznews*. Retrieved June 19, 2021, from https://www.biznews.com/thought-leaders/2021/04/24/unemployment-south-africa

Hope, K. R. (2000). *Corruption and development in Africa*. In K. R. Hope & B. C. Chikulo (Eds.), *Corruption and development in Africa* (pp. 17–39). Palgrave Macmillan.

Hunter, Q. (2020). Podcast: 'Thuma Mina was meant for Zuma. Retrieved October 8, 2021, from https://www.timeslive.co.za/sunday-times/books/news/2020-01-10-podcast-thuma-mina-was-meant-for-jacobzuma/

Imiera, P. P. (2020). The corruption race in Africa: Nigeria versus South Africa, who cleans the mess first? *De Jure Law Journal, 53*(1), 70–89. https://doi.org/10.17159/2225-7160/2020/v53a5

Jones, C. (2021). Corruption is crippling Africa, 'more like sand than oil in the economic engine.' *Daily Maverick*. Retrieved June 13, 2021, from https://www.dailymaverick.co.za/opinionista/2021-07-06-corruption-is-crippling-africa-more-like-sand-than-oil-in-the-economic-engine/

Ka-Ndyalvan, D. (2018). Thuma Mina: A spirit of self-conviction that brought colonial apartheid to its knees. *Daily Maverick*. Retrieved June 2, 2021, from https://www.dailymaverick.co.za/opinionista/2018-05-21-thuma-mina-a-spirit-of-self-conviction-that-brought-colonial-apartheid-to-its-knees/

Kgosana, R. (2018). 'Thuma mina' encourages Anglo American to invest R71.5bn. *The Citizen*. Retrieved June 20, 2021, from https://citizen.co.za/business/2028508/thuma-mina-encourages-anglo-american-to-invest-r71-5bn/

Khoza, A. (2018). Ramaphosa launches YES initiative to address youth unemployment. *News24*. Retrieved June 8, 2021, from https://www.news24.com/fin24/economy/ramaphosa-launches-yes-initiative-to-address-youth-unemployment-20180327

Kirkpatrick, S., & Locke, E. A. (1991). Leadership: Do traits matter? *Executive, 5*(2), 48–60. https://doi.org/10.2307/4165007

Kloppers, E. (2020). Performing the sacred – Aspects of singing and contextualisation in South Africa. *HTS Teologiese Studies/Theological Studies, 76*(2), a5477. https://doi.org/10.4102/hts.v76i2.5477

Lediga, S. (2018). The Thuma Mina programme is meant for all of us, not just the ANC. *Daily Maverick*. Retrieved May 25, 2021, from https://www.dailymaverick.co.za/opinionista/2018-05-22-the-thuma-mina-programme-is-meant-for-all-of-us-not-just-the-anc/

Mail & Guardian. (2019). Editorial: The destruction of Thuma Mina. *Mail & Guardian*. Retrieved June 2, 2021, from https://mg.co.za/article/2019-03-22-00-editorial-the-destruction-of-thuma-mina/

Maluleke, T. (2018). Op-Ed: The deep roots of Ramaphosa's 'Thuma Mina. *Daily Maverick*. Retrieved June 10, 2021, from https://www.Dailymaverick.co.za/article/2018-02-22-op-ed-the-deep-roots-of-ramaphosas-thuma-mina/#gsc.tab=0

Markle, A., & Cilliers, J. (2020). South Africa first! Getting to Thuma Mina. *ISS Southern Africa Report, 2020*(36), 1–44.

Martin, S. (2018). Thuma Mina – A new beginning for South Africa? Retrieved June 21, 2021, from https://politicaltheology.com/thuma-mina-a-new-beginning-for-south-africa/

Mashau, T. D., & Kgatle, M. S. (2021). Thuma Mina: A critical discourse on the prospect of a Ramaphosa presidency through the lenses of Isaiah 6:8. *Verbum et Ecclesia, 42*(1), a2129. https://doi.org/10.4102/ve.v42i1.2129

Mbaku, J. M. (2010). *Corruption in Africa: Causes, consequences, and cleanups.* Lexington Books.

Meylahn, J. A., & Musiyambiri, J. (2017). Ubuntu leadership in conversation with servant leadership in the Anglican Church: A case of Kunonga. *HTS Theological Studies, 73*(2), 1–6. https://doi.org/10.4102/hts.v73i2.4509

Mjo, O. (2018). Cyril Ramaphosa's 2018 Thuma Mina moments. *Timeslive.* Retrieved June 19, 2021, from https://www.timeslive.co.za/news/south-africa/2018-12-20-cyril-ramaphosas-2018-thuma-mina-moments/

Musixmatch. (n.d.). Here I am Lord by Ron feat. Shelly Hamilton. *Musixmatch.* Retrieved June 5, 2021, from https://www.musixmatch.com/lyrics/Ron-Hamilton-feat-Shelly-Hamilton/Here-Am-I-Lord

Nagel, A. (2020). Musicians take back power from politicians with 'the People's Version' of 'Thuma Mina'. *Sunday Times.* Retrieved May 26, 2021, from https://www.timeslive.co.za/sunday-times/lifestyle/2020-09-20-watch-musicians-take-back-power-from-politicians-with-the-peoples-version-of-thuma-mina/

Njilo, N. (2021). We will build an ethical ANC that acts against corruption without fear or favour: Paul Mashatile. *Timeslive.* Retrieved June 26, 2021, from https://www.timeslive.co.za/politics/2021-06-21-we-will-build-an-ethical-anc-that-acts-against-corruption-without-fear-or-favour-paul-mashatile/

Nzimakwe, T. I. (2014). Practising Ubuntu and leadership for good governance: The South African and continental dialogue. *African Journal of Public Affairs, 7*(4), 30–41.

Olivier de Sardan, J. P. (1999). A moral economy of corruption in Africa. *The Journal of Modern African Studies, 37*(1), 25–52.

Omarjee, L. (2021). SOEs were the 'honey pots' of state capture – But we will find the stolen money, Gordhan vows. *News24.* Retrieved June 20, 2021, from https://www.news24.com/fin24/economy/south-africa/soes-were-the-honey-pots-of-state-capture-but-we-will-find-the-stolen-money-gordhan-vows-20210216

Ondrová, D. (2016). Appeal of ethical accountability in public administration. *Rocznik Administracji Publicznej, 2*, 395–410.

Oxford, T. (2018). Putting Thuma Mina into action. *Mail & Guardian.* Retrieved June 2, 2021, from https://mg.co.za/article/2018-10-26-00-putting-thuma-mina-into-action/

Polity. (2018). SA: Ayanda Dlodlo: Address by Minister of Public Services and Administration, at the launch of the 2018 public service month, Velmore Conference Centre, Tshwane (31/08/2018). Retrieved June 12, 2021, from https://www.polity.org.za/article/sa-ayanda-dlodlo-address-by-minister-of-public-services-and-administration-at-the-launch-of-the-2018-public-service-month-velmore-conference-centre-tshwane-31082018-2018-08-31

Public Protector. (2016). State of Capture Report No 6 of 2016/17. *Public Protector.* Retrieved June 10, 2021, from http://www.pprotect.org/library/investigationreport/201617/StateCapture14October2016.pdf

Reddy, M. C. (2019). Thuma Mina. *CIGFARO Journal (Chartered Institute of Government Finance Audit and Risk Officers), 19*(4), 8–9. Retrieved June 7, 2021, from https://hdl.handle.net/10520/EJC-190d9c3e49

Shambala. (2020). 'Thuma Mina': Inspiring us to serve. *Shambala Private Game Reserve.* Retrieved June 16, 2021, from https://shambalaprivategamereserve.co.za/2020/06/19/thuma-mina-inspiring-us-to-serve/

Shange, Z. (2019). 'Yes, South Africa, Thuma Mina': Highlights from Ramaphosa's inauguration Speech. *Eyewitness News.* Retrieved June 7, 2021, from https://ewn.co.za/2019/05/25/yes-south-africa-thuma-mina-highlights-from-ramaphosa-s-first-speech-as-sa-president

South African Government News Agency. (2018). Public servants urged to be top service provider. *Sannews.* Retrieved June 21, 2021, from https://www.sanews.gov.za/south-africa/public-servants-urged-be-top-service-provider

Thamm, M. (2018). Thuma Mina: How Hugh Masekela, music and culture can help shape a new zeitgeist and Vision. *Daily Maverick.* Retrieved May 25, 2021, from https://www.dailymaverick.co.za/article/2018-02-19-thuma-mina-how-hugh-masekela-music-and-culture-can-help-us-shape-a-new-zeitgeist-and-vision/

Timeslive. (2019). President Cyril Ramaphosa's state of the nation address. *Timeslive.* Retrieved June 15, 2021, from https://www.timeslive.co.za/politics/2019-02-07-in-full%2D%2Dread-president-cyril-ramaphosas-state-of-the-nation-address/

# Part II

## Governance and Public Sector Performance

# 6

# African Ethics and Public Governance: Nepotism, Preferential Hiring, and Other Partiality

## Introduction

Most political and economic philosophy in the English language is grounded on Western moral theories, such as utilitarianism and Kantianism, which presume that the basic aim of a state should be to maximise benefit for its residents and respect their autonomy, respectively (e.g., Kymlicka, 2002). What form might political philosophy take if it appealed instead to an African moral theory different from the West's?

This chapter describes a moral principle informed by characteristically African values and applies it to how a state bureaucrat should distribute resources at a domestic level. It is a normative essay aimed at providing a convincing comprehensive account of how a government official in a post-independence sub-Saharan African country should make decisions about how to allocate goods such as civil service jobs and contracts with private firms. Should such a person refrain from considering any

T. Metz (✉)
University of Pretoria, Pretoria, South Africa
e-mail: th.metz@up.ac.za

© The Author(s), under exclusive license to Springer Nature Switzerland AG 2022
K. Ogunyemi et al. (eds.), *Ethics and Accountable Governance in Africa's Public Sector,
Volume I*, Palgrave Studies of Public Sector Management in Africa,
https://doi.org/10.1007/978-3-030-95394-2_6

**109**

particulars about potential recipients, or might it be appropriate to consider, for example, family membership, party affiliation, race, or revolutionary stature as reasons to benefit certain individuals at some cost to the public? Which of these factors should be considered an unjust or corrupt basis on which to allocate state goods and which should not?

As described in more detail below, those called "impartialists" in this chapter answer by saying that officials working for an African state should always act only for the sake of the whole society. When awarding a job or contract, the only consideration is whether it is in the public interest. By contrast, those labelled "partialists" claim that civil servants may act for the sake of certain individuals at some foreseeable cost to the society. From this perspective, it can be right for civil servants to consider certain features of those being awarded the job or contract other than their ability to serve the public, say, the fact of them having suffered historical injustice or perhaps being members of the same political party.

This chapter outlines an attractive moral theory with African content that forbids both impartialism and a strong form of partialism according to which government officials may favour members of their families or political parties. Between these two extremes, a "moderate partialism" is prescribed. This approach permits government agents to favour, at some cost to the public, veterans and victims of state injustices, but not those in their family or party. This chapter seeks to provide a new, unified explanation of why characteristically sub-Saharan African values permit some forms of partiality, such as the preferential hiring of those who suffered from or struggled against colonialism, but forbid other forms such as nepotism, whereby officials use state resources to benefit family members at the expense of the public, and also what is often called "prebendalism," whereby they benefit members of an ethnic, religious, political, or other group related to them (Joseph, 2013, pp. 263–265).

In so doing, this chapter suggests that African political philosophers and policy makers need not appeal to Western or other foreign moral systems for a principled foundation for good governance in contemporary African states. It draws on a recognisably African morality to offer principled guidance to officials in sub-Saharan African governments about how to allocate resources such as jobs and contracts. Corruption is one (but not the only) major reason why sub-Saharan African societies have not developed as they might have since independence.[1] Sometimes African values are even invoked to justify behaviour that this chapter deems unjust (as is mentioned in Gyekye, 1997, pp. 196, 252–257; de Sardan, 1999; Ramose, 2003, p. 329). For instance, believing in the African dictum that "charity begins at home," some officials rig tender processes so that extended family members who are in business win contracts with the state. This chapter argues that an attractive African ethic forbids such strong partialism as corrupt, while permitting other forms of partiality such as affirmative action for veterans.[2] Although both nepotism and affirmative action would normally involve picking less than the best qualified to serve the public, this chapter contends that certain communal values salient in Africa forbid the former but permit the latter.

This chapter is a work of political philosophy, not political science. It is a strictly normative enterprise, aimed at justifying or, alternately, proscribing certain state practices by drawing out the implications of a principle of right action informed by salient sub-Saharan African values. It is not an empirical project attempting to recount or explain the behaviour of any sub-Saharan African state or its officials. Furthermore, it remains relatively abstract, in the sense of operating at the level of principles and their implications, and not making concrete policy recommendations about how a particular African state should change.[3]

The chapter begins by defining in more detail the debate between impartialism, strong partialism, and moderate partialism. The following part then describes an attractive African moral theory used to evaluate

---

[1] According to one estimate, if corruption in sub-Saharan Africa were simply on par with the world average, as opposed to much worse than it, GDP could increase 1 or 2 percent each year (Sobrinho & Thakoor, 2019, p. 35).

[2] To judge certain practices to be morally wrong does not necessarily mean that one should view corruption as a problem centrally to be addressed by, say, improving individual character, as Gyekye (2013), Dudzai (2021), and to some extent Genger (2018) do. It is consistent to hold that the wrongness of corruption is to be rebutted principally through structural reforms of certain kinds, such as those discussed in Dumisa and Amao (2015), Hope (2017), and Olanipekun (2021), and not so much the moral education of individuals.

[3] Arguing that there is something morally objectionable about nepotism and prebendalism is consistent with questioning the West's motivations for intervention into African political processes to address corruption as well as its likely outcomes (on which see De Maria, 2007). Explaining precisely why a practice is wrong is one thing, while holding a certain view about who should address it (and how) is another.

these approaches. The preferred philosophical interpretation of African values is communal, placing harmonious or friendly relationships at the heart of right action. The rest of the chapter applies this relational ethic to decisions that sub-Saharan African state officials should make when allocating jobs and contracts. It argues that the ethic forbids officials from favouring people related *to them*, but it permits them to favour people related *to the state* in certain ways. The conclusion gives a summary highlighting key points of use for future normative theorising on African politics.

## Impartialism Versus Partialism

Recall the major positions that this essay seeks to evaluate. What this essay dubs "impartialism" is the view that a government official in sub-Saharan Africa should act only for the sake of the public, never for individuals in the light of their characteristics such as being members of a family or a historically disadvantaged group. For the impartialist, when a civil servant needs to award a job or a contract, the only consideration should be the candidates' qualifications, that is, the extent to which they could help to carry out the state's duty to serve the public. For instance, qualifications for a job would normally include education, intelligence, experience, and disposition to work hard. These traits are ones that would most promote the public interest.

What is called "partialism" here is the rejection of impartialism, and hence is the view that a government official should sometimes act to benefit some individual or group at some foreseeable cost to the public. For the partialist, when a civil servant needs to award a job or a contract, they should take into account something in addition to qualifications to serve the public and hence be willing to give it to someone who is less than the best qualified (even if minimally or satisfactorily so). For example, strong partialism allows an official to award a job or contract to people at least partly because they are related to him through, say, family or political party. Moderate partialism forbids that but allows (and perhaps even requires) an official to award a job or contract to people at least partly because they are related to the state, such as veterans.

These views are competing answers to the question of whether and, if so, how an official in a sub-Saharan African government may distribute state resources in order to benefit certain individuals living within the state at some cost to the public. Focus on this question means setting aside others. For instance, this chapter does not address the dispute between cosmopolitans, who defend a state that ignores borders in its fundamental distributive policy, and nationalists, who defend one that gives priority to the interests of legal residents (see Tan, 2004). The key issues here are how domestic resources should be utilised, not how big they should be compared with resources directed at foreign policy objectives.

Furthermore, this chapter ignores the debate on whether the state would best serve the public interest by promoting a certain conception of the good life. It does not enquire whether the state should be politically liberal in the sense of refraining from deliberately fostering a certain way of life and thereby letting people choose their own lifestyles (see Zellentin, 2012). Setting aside what counts as the public interest, this chapter instead considers whether state officials may seek to promote it (however it is best conceived) to less than the maximum degree for the sake of certain individuals such as family members or veterans.

In referring to state (or government) officials and resources, this chapter addresses bureaucrats such as the human resources officers who award government jobs and the procurement officers who award contracts to private firms on tender. A broader reading of government officials and resources for allocation might include legislators, who decide how to use taxpayers' money. Although the position developed here probably has implications for such politicians, it does not address them.[4]

The rest of this chapter argues that a plausible African moral theory supports moderate partialism, rejecting both impartialism and strong partialism. It shows that acceptance of affirmative action and rejection of nepotism both follow from a certain philosophical interpretation of sub-Saharan African values.

---

[4] In the original, longer version of this essay, it is argued that the principles advanced here entail that a legislator ought not to act for the sake of their constituency and instead for the sake of the public as a whole (Metz, 2009, p. 348).

# African Moral Theory

In its appeal to African values, this chapter invokes an understanding of them in the form of a moral theory. A moral theory is a fundamental principle that is meant to account for what right actions, as distinct from wrong, have in common. It is a single principle that purports to entail and explain all permissible decisions, as contrasted with those that are not morally permitted. Familiar examples from modern Western philosophy include the principle of utility, that an act or policy is wrong in so far as it fails to improve the average quality of life, and the principle of respect for autonomy, that an act or policy is wrong insofar as it degrades people's ability to act based on their own rational reflection (see Kymlicka, 2002, esp. pp. 10–153).

Now, a moral theory counts as African if it is informed, not so much by Western cultures, but rather by many of the long-standing ethical beliefs and practices of a variety of peoples in the large sub-Saharan African region.[5] To deem a moral theory African does not therefore imply that all societies on the continent have believed it or, indeed, that any has been aware of it. The following ethical principle is a philosophical construction unifying a wide array of the moral judgements and ways of life found among many of the cultures indigenous to the sub-Saharan African region.

Here is a basic statement of the African moral theory this chapter employs to appraise the debate between impartialism and partialism: an act is right just in so far it is a way of honouring people's capacity to relate harmoniously (or communally), that is, to be party to relationships in which people identify and exhibit solidarity with one another. An action is wrong if and only if it fails to respect people's dignified ability to commune (or harmonise) with others and to be communed (harmonised) with by them.

To begin to unpack this terse statement, consider that many indigenous sub-Saharan Africans would sum up morality with the phrase, "A person is a person through other persons" (Nkulu-N'Sengha, 2009; see

---

[5] For further articulation and defence of this way of understanding the meaning of "African" and other geographical labels, see Metz (2015).

also Ramose, 2003, p. 385). To the foreign English speaker, this maxim means little, initially suggesting banal ideas about how children are causally dependent on adults to survive. However, what it expresses is best interpreted as including a rich and specific understanding of how people should treat one another. When Africans make this claim they are indicating, in part, that the only way to develop moral personhood, that is, to become a virtuous agent or lead a genuinely human life, is to interact with others in a certain positive way (Nkulu-N'Sengha, 2009).

The relevant way to relate is often characterised in terms of harmony or entering into community, or at least that is prominent among indigenous southern African interpretations of morality, on which this chapter particularly draws. For instance, Archbishop Desmond Tutu, winner of the Nobel Peace Prize (in 1984) and renowned leader of South Africa's Truth and Reconciliation Commission, sums up one major strand of African ethical thinking this way:

> We say, "a person is a person through other people." It is not "I think therefore I am." It says rather: "I am human because I belong." I participate, I share....Harmony, friendliness, community are great goods. Social harmony is for us the *summum bonum*—the greatest good. (Tutu, 1999, p. 35)

Similarly, Yvonne Mokgoro, a former Constitutional Court Justice in South Africa, says that

> harmony is achieved through close and sympathetic social relations within the group—thus the notion *umuntu ngumuntu ngabantu* (a person is a person through other persons—ed.) ... which also implies that during one's lifetime, one is constantly challenged by others, practically, to achieve self-fulfilment through ... a morality of co-operation, compassion, communalism. (Mokgoro, 1998, p. 17)

Notice that, for both thinkers, one is to realise oneself or become a genuine human being and to do that by prizing harmonious or communal relationships, ones in which one not only is close to and participates with others, but also shares with others and sympathises with them.

These views are about moral virtue in the first instance and not right action. They are accounts of how to be a good person, and not so much about which public policy would be just. However, it is not a stretch to interpret them in ways that could compete with Western accounts of right and wrong, for example, in terms of what reduces the general welfare in the long run (utilitarianism) or what degrades the autonomy of persons (Kantianism), at least upon adding in the idea that human persons have a dignity that must be treated with respect. This, too, is a salient idea in African moral thought (e.g., Cobbah, 1987; Deng, 2004; Iroegbu, 2005; Gyekye, 2010, sec. 6). A good explanation of why a good person is one who harmonises or communes with other persons is that people have a dignity in virtue of their ability to harmonise and be harmonised with, which demands respectful treatment that normally takes the form of being related to harmoniously.

As Tutu and Mokgoro implicitly suggest, harmonious or communal relationships are not merely those of any stable, peaceful group. A dictator whose subjects do not rebel because they are afraid does not have a harmonious relationship with them in the relevant, morally attractive sense. The harmony to be prized is a way of relating in which people both identify and exhibit solidarity with one another, which a dictator fails to do. Consider these elements in more detail.

To identify with other people consists of two main things. First, it includes being close in the sense of sharing a common sense of self or thinking as a member of a group or part of a relationship. Instead of thinking of oneself as an "I," distinct from and perhaps even above others, the self becomes part of a "we," enjoying a sense of togetherness. For example, a person who identifies with colleagues in an academic department speaks of "us," gladly thinking of himself as part of a group. Second, identifying with others also includes participating with them on even-handed terms. One engages in joint projects in which people cooperate to achieve shared or at least compatible ends. Another facet of academic collegiality, for example, is striving together with other department members to advance teaching and research. Failing to identify with others could take an extreme, divisive form in which one has an attitude of "me versus you" and subordinates other people to achieve one's ends.

Beyond identifying with others, a harmonious or communal relationship also consists of exhibiting solidarity towards them. This is a matter of being positively oriented towards others' interests or caring for them, in a word. Such behaviour includes helping other people by sharing one's labour and money to meet their needs and, furthermore, doing so for their sake. It also includes acting out of sympathy with others, for instance, choosing in ways consistent with being happy when others flourish and sad when they fail. Failing to exhibit solidarity could take an extreme form of ill-will, involving doing harm to others and acting consequent to taking pleasure in their pain.

Although relationships of identity and solidarity are often found together, they are distinct in principle and sometimes come apart in practice. For example, people might identify with others but not exhibit solidarity with them, as in the relationship between workers and management in many capitalist firms. Furthermore, people might exhibit solidarity towards others without identifying with them, as when making anonymous donations to charity. However, a characteristically African understanding of morality instructs an agent to treat people with respect by, wherever possible (with innocent parties), exhibiting both identity and solidarity, that is, enjoying a sense of togetherness and engaging in cooperative projects as well as helping others and doing so out of sympathy with them.

Wrong actions, by this present ethic, are those that degrade people's capacity to be party to harmonious (communal) relationships and typically take the form of discordant (anti-social) behaviour directed towards those who have not been initially discordant. According to this moral theory, the reason that it is immoral to kidnap, rape, steal, lie, or exploit is that such actions characteristically: treat others as separate and inferior, as opposed to bound up with oneself; subordinate others, instead of coordinate in pursuit of compatible aims; reduce others' quality of life, instead of meeting their needs; and are indifferent, or even hostile, towards others' interests, instead of being consistent with sympathy and altruism. When we fail to harmonise with other innocents, and especially when we act discordantly towards them in the above ways, we are degrading them, treating their capacity to be party to harmonious relationships as either non-existent or unimportant. This account of what makes an act wrong is a plausible alternative to the ideas that they tend to cause long-term harm as opposed to benefit (utilitarianism) or involve treating people's capacity for autonomy disrespectfully (Kantianism).

This relational interpretation of right and wrong action is informed by salient features of many sub-Saharan African peoples.[6] For example, they often think society should be akin to family. They tend to believe in the importance of greeting those one encounters, including strangers. They typically refer to people beyond the nuclear family with titles such as "sister" and "father." They frequently believe that ritual and tradition have moral significance. They tend to think there is some obligation to wed and procreate. They usually do not believe that retribution is a proper aim of criminal justice, inclining towards reconciliation. They commonly think there is a strong duty for the rich to aid the poor. Finally, for now, they often value consensus in decision-making, seeking unanimous agreement and not resting content with majority rule. The prescription to respect people's capacity to harmonise and be harmonised with entails living in these ways. Their moral worth is plausibly understood as instances of identity and solidarity.

Some might like to see here a full-blown defence of the Afro-communal principle. They might want reason to think it the best possible articulation of an African perspective on ethics, or even the most attractive conception of morality in general. This chapter lacks the scope for either (see Metz, 2021). Instead, it is merely articulating one prima facie attractive moral theory informed by characteristically sub-Saharan African values, which is now applied to the way a civil servant should allocate resources such as government jobs or contracts. A utilitarian would do so in whichever way would best promote the general welfare in the future. A Kantian would do so in a manner that respects people's capacity for autonomous decision-making. These two principles would seemingly rule out nepotism and other corrupt practices as either harmful to, or disrespectful of, the public. What, now, about an African ethic grounded on communal ideals? What does it have to say about when the allocation of resources by a civil servant is unjust?

---

[6] The following is a brief statement, while a much fuller one is in Metz (2021, pp. 50-60, 123-136), from which the rest of this paragraph tersely draws.

# Against Strong Partialism

This chapter aims to establish that the African moral theory articulated above prescribes a moderate partialism, the view that government officials should distribute resources to benefit the public as a whole, except where individuals have had a certain relationship with the state, such as by having made great sacrifices for it (as veterans or freedom fighters) or having been seriously wronged by it (as historically disadvantaged individuals). In this section, it is argued that this African ethic rules out a stronger partialism whereby government officials may act to the benefit of individuals related to them as, say, members of their family, ethnic group, or political party.

To begin, note that there is nothing in the African moral theory to permit government officials to distribute resources to benefit themselves. A demand to honour others in virtue of their dignified capacity for relationships of identity and solidarity clearly forbids procurement officials from awarding a contract to a firm to receive a kickback. Instead, they are obligated to harmonise with other innocent parties, which means fostering other people's ends and advancing their good.

However, even if the African ethic forbids using state resources for private gain, such that "people first" should be the motto of a civil servant,[7] it is not obvious which other people should come first. As mentioned above, some interpret African morality to allow, and perhaps even require, civil servants to use state resources for the benefit of their family. African values are commonly deemed to presume that family comes first or that charity begins at home, and even those sympathetic to other moral principles will find compelling the general idea that loved ones normally take priority over strangers. Why should an ethic that values communal or harmonious relationships forbid civil servants from showing preferential treatment towards those who are closest to them?

To answer, note first that the African ethic sketched above is comprehensive, intended to provide a standard of moral correctness for

---

[7] In South Africa, *batho pele*, which means people first, has been a maxim promulgated to guide the behaviour of civil servants (Department of Social Development of the Republic of South Africa, 2021). How well it has been observed is contentious.

individuals and institutions. Thus, this theory can be used to morally appraise the decisions and policies of organisations such as corporations and schools. Applying it to a twenty-first-century African state, what does the ethic entail for the way it ought to allocate public resources?

The straightforward answer is "not in a very partial manner." A state that is strongly partial would inadequately realise harmony between itself and those living within its territory. It would fail to treat each citizen as having a dignity in virtue of (in part) their ability to be the object of a communal relationship. A state that routinely distributed resources to benefit its officials' relatives, knowing that this would cost the public, would do a poor job of developing identity and solidarity with each legal resident. Such a state would identify with only a small portion of the public, failing to conceive of itself as part of a "we" with the population as a whole and coercing the mass of citizens into paying taxes that end up benefiting the relatives of a few government officials. In addition, such a state would be exhibiting solidarity towards only a small, select group and acting uncaringly towards the greater population.

Furthermore, in failing to exhibit identity and solidarity with the public, much of the public, in turn, would fail to exhibit identity and solidarity with the state. For example, those who do not benefit from the nepotism would naturally come to view the state as apart from them. They would be inclined to undermine it with protests and other forms of civil unrest. Such behaviour by the state would not encourage citizens to enjoy a common sense of self with the state or to go out of their way to support state projects. South Africa during apartheid, as well as prebendalist behaviour by post-independence political elites, illustrates clearly how a strongly partial state both fails to harmonise with everyone in its territory and also generates discord.

Now, the state can manifest harmony with the public and avoid being strongly partial only if its officials are not strongly partial themselves when they make decisions on the state's behalf. It follows, therefore, that state officials must not make strongly partial decisions in their public lives. A procurement official who awards a contract to members of his family or political party, without considering whether they are eligible or will otherwise do the requisite job, fails to secure the kind of state required by an ethic of respect for the dignity of each as capable of being party to harmonious relationships.

However, this section must go further, by explaining why a civil servant's duty not to be strongly partial is stronger than his duty to favour loved ones. Regarding the state as an institution, the African moral theory requires civil servants not to be strongly partial, but at the individual level, this theory might still appear to recommend being strongly partial. For example, one may and should save the life of one's child, rather than a stranger's, when such a situation of forced choice arises. A civil servant might then appear to be in conflict regarding their duties and in need of a clear reason why their duty to the public, by supporting a state that is not strongly partial, should outweigh that to their relatives.

The deep reason for a civil servant not to be strongly partial turns on the proper way to value personal relationships. If necessary, it would be acceptable to save a loved one before a stranger, but note that it would not be acceptable to save a loved one by killing a non-aggressive stranger. Imagine, for instance, that a loved one needed a new liver to survive and that the only way to acquire one were to kidnap an innocent person and forcibly extract one. No dignity-based ethic would permit such drastic action to promote the interests, even the urgent interests, of a loved one. The general principle is that respect for the dignified capacity to be party to harmonious relationships means that even long-standing and intense bonds generally should not be promoted by using a very discordant means towards innocents (Metz, 2021, pp. 113–117).

If that principle is sound, then it remains merely to point out that government officials who acted in a strongly partial, for example, nepotistic, way would be using a very discordant means to help those related to them. Each civil servant has a duty to help ensure that the state's behaviour is not strongly partial and instead identifies with and exhibits solidarity towards each citizen. If a civil servant shirks this duty, they exploit those colleagues and their relatives who have upheld their duties. They also exploit tax-paying citizens who all have a duty to facilitate a state that identifies and exhibits solidarity with each member of the public. Exploitation, or benefiting from others' sacrifice as if they existed merely to serve one's ends, is a discordant or anti-social way of relating to others. (In addition, sometimes state bureaucrats promise to serve the public or take an oath to do so, which, in that case, means there would be even more discord if they instead directed public resources towards private interests.)

Note that it will not suffice to say that nepotism is wrong simply because it is a matter of stealing; for to characterise it as stealing is merely to say that it is an unjustified taking, which begs the philosophical question of *why* it is unjustified. This chapter has argued that nepotism is unjustified mainly because the state is obligated to identify and exhibit solidarity with the public as a whole, which it could not do if its officials routinely acted nepotically. Any given official who uses public resources to satisfy private interests is therefore acting unfairly; they are exploiting their fellow officials who have not acted in that way, making an exception for themselves and treating themselves and their kin as more important than the others are. They would be promoting communal relationships by using an anti-social means, which the dignity-based principle rules out as disrespectful. Furthermore, if literally all officials happened to act in a similarly nepotistic way, then, although they would not be exploiting one another, they would be taking advantage of taxpayers who have done their duty to provide resources to facilitate a state that should harmonise with every member of the public.

In sum, the Afro-communal ethic forbids not only nepotism, but also any allocation of state resources to those related in some way to human resources or procurement officials, since doing so takes advantage of innocent parties such as fellow officials and taxpayers who have done their part to support a state that treats everyone with respect. However, that is not to conclude that state bureaucrats may never be partial in the way they distribute government jobs and contracts. A different kind of partiality does not threaten harmony and may even respect people's capacity for it, or so the next section argues.

## Against Impartialism

The previous section argued that strong partialism is forbidden in the interest of the whole public, which might suggest that impartialism is true, such that state officials should always act in ways they expect to benefit the whole public. However, this section argues that there is a kind of partialism that is morally appropriate. Basically, it argues that there is a significant moral difference between awarding jobs and contracts to those who are *related in some way to particular government officials*, on the one hand, and to those who are *related to the state* in certain ways, on the other. Here, it is argued that, according to the Afro-communal ethic, people such as veterans and victims of state injustice may, in principle, be given some degree of preference in the awarding of government jobs and contracts, which means that impartialism is an inappropriate way to allocate state resources. Even to those already convinced that African values permit preferential hiring, this section should be of interest since it brings out the unified basis, viz., the ethic of communal relationships, that forbids one kind of favouritism, namely, nepotism and prebendalism, but permits another, namely, affirmative action.

Consider the preferential treatment of veterans, those formally employed by the state to fight on its behalf or, alternatively, those freedom fighters and leaders of the struggle who opposed the state on behalf of the public it was once oppressing. In both cases, individuals risked life, limb, and livelihood to aid the state or the public. Communal relationships include showing gratitude to those who have worked for the benefit of others. A person who is able but not willing to thank someone who has provided above-satisfactory service is not properly recognising the other's dignified capacity to relate in a harmonious way. Ingratitude involves a person discordantly treating others as though they exist to serve them, which a harmonious relationship would, of course, exclude. Respecting people in virtue of their capacity for harmonious/communal relationships therefore requires the state to recognise those who have made great sacrifices for it or the public. That might mean giving some preference to veterans when awarding government contracts and jobs. "Some" is the key word here, for all decisions should still be based *largely*, even if not exclusively, on what would be good for the public in its entirety. This means that those selected for a contract or job must be adequately, even if not superlatively, qualified.

Similarly, the state may rightly give some preference to individuals from whom, in the past, it had demanded unjust sacrifices. Here, the relevant moral category is not gratitude but repentance. In a choice between making amends to a wronged friend or forgetting that one and, instead, going out to make a new friend, a dignity-based ethic that values communality demands the wrong to be set right first, presuming this were feasible. A person's duty is to mend any discordant relationships before forging new, harmonious ones (supposing both could not be done at the same time). This point applies not merely to individuals, but also to a state obligated to prize people because of their capacity for identity and solidarity. If a state has systematically wronged any of its citizens, such as South Africa under apartheid, respect for their communal nature would require an apology followed by a serious attempt to repair the broken relationship. One way for a state to express contrition and to correct its mistakes (in part) would be to give preference for government jobs and contracts to applicants from the sector it had wronged, even if they are somewhat less qualified and hence doing so would come at some cost to the public.

Space does not permit a complete defence of preferential hiring, but two objections based on the African ethic should be considered. First, it might be argued that it is wrong to make up with those whom one has wronged by wronging others (e.g., Fullinwider, 1980). That is, some might say that, even if preferential hiring of black people who had been discriminated against would express contrition and foster reconciliation, it would be objectionably discordant with respect to white people. Not being considered equally for government jobs and contracts might be viewed as divisive and a manifestation of ill-will by the state.

In reply, suppose that, in adopting preferential hiring, the state would indeed be somewhat discordant regarding those white people who were neither responsible for, nor beneficiaries of, past injustice. Then the degree to which preferential hiring wrongs them must be compared with the degree to which black people would be wronged were preferential hiring not adopted. It would be wrong to fail to apologise to those whom one had wronged, and also wrong not to try to mend a break in a relationship, were one at fault. Hence, the state would probably be doing an injustice, regardless of whether it adopted affirmative action or not, and, if so, then the state should minimise the injustice it does. It seems that to adopt affirmative action would be the lesser injustice, when the number of black people wronged is great and the wrongs done to them were serious, and when the number of white people is small and the burden on them is comparatively light, say, because they could likely obtain comparable resources elsewhere (cf. van Roojen, 1997).

Second, it might be argued that preferential hiring would foster long-term discord by worsening the public service offered by the state and causing disaffection such as might result from a strongly partial state (discussed in Edigheji, 2007). Were the state much less able to prevent crime and implement welfare programmes because of affirmative action and were it to alienate substantial portions of the public as a result, then it would fail to promote the proper degree of identity and solidarity regarding the public.

In response, it is true that the effects of preferential hiring on the public must be given moral consideration. Despite being against impartialism, this chapter accepts the idea that the primary obligation of state officials is to act for the sake of the public. There could be cases where the long-term consequences of affirmative action policies would be so deleterious to promoting relationships of identity and solidarity that they should not be adopted. The point is that, at the level of principle, the African moral theory allows state officials to take past sacrifice for the state, and past injustice by the state, as reason to act for some individuals or groups, even if it means not benefiting the public to the *maximum* available degree.

Hence, when it comes to service delivery, state officials may sometimes provide somewhat less than the best possible to the public, when doing so means giving advantage to individuals with certain relationships with the state, specifically veterans and historically disadvantaged individuals. By giving these persons only "some" preference for government jobs and contracts, and by requiring them to be adequately qualified, harm to public service would be unlikely to be substantial. On disaffection, the public is not likely to feel alienated from a government that gives preference to veterans, especially those who struggled on behalf of the public. A largely black public in sub-Saharan Africa is, of course, unlikely to feel as divided from a state that adopts affirmative action for black people as it would towards one awarding jobs and contracts to those arbitrarily related to government officials. Furthermore, even if whites felt alienated from a state that gave some preference to blacks, they would be largely unjustified in the many cases where they had benefited greatly from past injustice and the current imposition upon them were small. The prospect of irrational disaffection does matter morally, for any disaffection means failure to identify with the state, but it does not matter greatly. In friendships, some allowance should be made for the irrationalities of a friend, and conflict grounded on unreasonable expectations or reactions should be avoided, but there is no obligation to indulge.

There are other possible objections to these arguments for preferential hiring or to preferential hiring itself. This chapter has not demonstrated, for example, that a necessary way to express gratitude to veterans, and to express remorse and mend rifts with those wronged during colonialism, would be to adopt preferential hiring. It has at best shown that preferential hiring would be one way to discharge these obligations. However, it is not the aim of this chapter to provide a complete defence of preferential hiring. Instead, it takes a certain interpretation of African ethics for granted and teases out some of its likely implications for how to allocate state resources. It argues that an African ethic prescribing respect for people's communal nature would, in many cases, permit preferential hiring of the sort described and for reasons that should be taken seriously.

# Conclusion

This chapter has sought to answer the question of how human resources and procurement officials in a sub-Saharan African state should award government contracts and jobs. It has asked specifically whether they should do so impartially, invariably for the sake of the public as a whole, or whether they may do so partially on occasion and, if so, in what respect. To answer, the chapter has appealed to a moral theory informed by African values that contrasts with utilitarian and Kantian approaches to justice. This moral theory requires respect for people because of their dignified capacity for harmonious relationships, where such relationships are a matter of identifying with others and exhibiting solidarity with them. The chapter has argued that such a moral theory provides a unified and plausible way to account for the various duties binding on officials regarding the use of state resources.

Specifically, the ethic has been shown to forbid state officials from awarding resources to individuals because they are *related to them* through membership in the same family, ethnic group, or political party. Allocating resources in that strongly partial way would be exploitative, and hence degradingly use a discordant means to foster harmony among associates. However, the ethic does not require state officials to award resources on an utterly impartial basis; they may favour individuals with certain *relationships with the state*, specifically, veterans and victims of state injustice, even when it would cost the public something. Honouring people's social nature requires displaying gratitude, expressing remorse, and trying to reconcile with those the state has been wronged, all of which the state could achieve by preferential hiring and without promoting substantial discord in society as a result.

Several of the points made in this chapter should be useful in addressing additional political, legal, economic, and social issues from an African perspective. For instance, it should be of value to understand the following distinctions: between an African moral theory that prizes harmony and a Western one that values welfare or agency; between different facets of harmony, viz., identity and solidarity; between institutions and individuals as objects of moral appraisal; between valuing relationships with an institution and relationships with those within an institution; and between the desirable end of a harmonious (communal) relationship and the impermissible means of a discordant (anti-social) one. These theoretical resources should be useful when applying African values to other domains.

It is hoped that African moral and political philosophy will develop alongside African economies and societies. More strongly, it is hoped that African economies and societies will develop in part because of the development of African moral and political philosophy.[8]

---

[8] For written comments on a previous draft, thanks are due to Mfuniselwa Bhengu, Stephen Kershnar, Munyaradzi Murove, Pedro Tabensky, and two anonymous reviewers for Palgrave Macmillan. This chapter is published with the generous permission of the University of KwaZulu-Natal Press and is a shortened and modified excerpt from Metz (2009).

# References

Cobbah, J. (1987). African values and the human rights debate. *Human Rights Quarterly, 9*(3), 309–331.

De Maria, W. (2007). Does African "corruption" exist? *African Journal of Business Ethics, 2*(1), 1–9.

de Sardan, J. P. O. (1999). A moral economy of corruption in Africa? *Journal of Modern African Studies, 37*(1), 25–52.

Deng, F. (2004). Human rights in the African context. In K. Wiredu (Ed.), *A companion to African philosophy* (pp. 499–508). Blackwell.

Department of Social Development of the Republic of South Africa. (2021). *Batho pele.* https://www.dsd.gov.za/index.php/about/batho-pele

Dudzai, C. (2021). The value of Ubuntu towards the fight against corruption in Zimbabwe. *African Journal of Social Work, 11*(1), 48–51.

Dumisa, S., & Amao, O. B. (2015). The utility of moral philosophy and professional ethics in the fight against corruption in South Africa: Any role for Ubuntu? *Ubuntu: Journal of Conflict and Social Transformation, 4*(1), 83–109.

Edigheji, O. (2007). Affirmative action and state capacity in a democratic South Africa. *Policy: Issues & Actors, 20*(4), 1–13. https://media.africaportal.org/documents/pia20_4.pdf

Fullinwider, R. (1980). *The reverse discrimination controversy.* Rowman and Littlefield.

Genger, P. (2018). Combating corruption with African restorative justice tradition. *African Journal of Criminology and Justice Studies, 11*(1), 20–40.

Gyekye, K. (1997). *Tradition and modernity: Philosophical reflections on the African experience.* Oxford University Press.

Gyekye, K. (2010). African ethics. In E. Zalta (Ed.), *The Stanford encyclopedia of philosophy.* http://plato.stanford.edu/archives/fall2010/entries/african-ethics/

Gyekye, K. (2013). Political corruption as an essentially moral problem. In K. Gyekye (Ed.), *Philosophy, culture and vision: African perspectives* (pp. 82–116). Sub-Saharan Publishers.

Hope, K. R. (2017). *Corruption and governance in Africa.* Palgrave Macmillan.

Iroegbu, P. (2005). Right to life and the means to life. In P. Iroegbu & A. Echekwube (Eds.), *Kpim of morality ethics* (pp. 446–449). Heinemann Educational Books.

Joseph, R. (2013). Epilogue: The logic and legacy of prebendalism in Nigeria. In W. Adebanwi & E. Obadare (Eds.), *Democracy and prebendalism in Nigeria* (pp. 261–279). Palgrave Macmillan.

Kymlicka, W. (2002). *Contemporary political philosophy* (2nd ed.). Oxford University Press.

Metz, T. (2009). African moral theory and public governance. In M. F. Murove (Ed.), *African ethics: An anthology of comparative and applied ethics* (pp. 335–356). University of KwaZulu-Natal Press.

Metz, T. (2015). How the West was one: The western as individualist, the African as communitarian. *Educational Philosophy and Theory, 47*(11), 1175–1184.

Metz, T. (2021). *A relational moral theory: African ethics in and beyond the continent.* Oxford University Press.

Mokgoro, Y. (1998). *Ubuntu* and the law in South Africa. *Potchefstroom Electronic Law Journal, 1*(1), 15–26.

Nkulu-N'Sengha, M. (2009). *Bumuntu.* In M. K. Asante & A. Mazama (Eds.), *Encyclopedia of African religion* (pp. 142–147). Sage.

Olanipekun, O. V. (2021). Political corruption in Africa: Revisiting Kwame Gyekye's moral solution. *The African Review, 48*(1), 122–139.

Ramose, M. (2003). The ethics of Ubuntu. In P. H. Coetzee & A. P. J. Roux (Eds.), *Philosophy from Africa* (2nd ed., pp. 324–330). Oxford University Press.

Sobrinho, N., & Thakoor, V. (2019). More sand than oil. *Finance & Development, 56*(3), 35–37.

Tan, K.-C. (2004). *Justice without borders: Cosmopolitanism, nationalism, and patriotism.* Cambridge University Press.

Tutu, D. (1999). *No future without forgiveness.* Random House.

Van Roojen, M. (1997). Affirmative action, non-consequentialism, and responsibility for the effects of past discrimination. *Public Affairs Quarterly, 11*(3), 281–301.

Zellentin, A. (2012). *Liberal neutrality.* De Gruyter.

# 7

# Anti-corruption Initiatives in Africa's Public Sector

Samuel Wenyah

## Introduction

The battle against corruption in Africa is a deep-rooted cliché, enshrined into the very fabric of the African society. Corruption is not peculiar to only Africa, but its existence is intertwined with the misfortunes of the continent (Lambsdorff, 2007; Rose-Ackerman & Soreide, 2011). Corruption has proved to be a longer-term threat to peace, justice, and sustainable development, and its pervasive nature enables it to be a constant presence in every aspect of our daily lives (IMF, 2016; World Bank, 2015). Its terrible consequences continue to wreak havoc on every sector of the economy, including both public and private administrations (UNECA, 2011). According to *Quartz Africa* (2020), citing a report from the United Nations, it is estimated that Africa loses US$88 billion yearly to corruption. This is approximately 3.7 per cent of Africa's total Gross Domestic Product (GDP) and directly proportional to the total GDP of Uganda, Sudan, and Mali combined.

S. Wenyah (✉)
University of Ghana, Accra, Ghana

© The Author(s), under exclusive license to Springer Nature Switzerland AG 2022    **131**
K. Ogunyemi et al. (eds.), *Ethics and Accountable Governance in Africa's Public Sector,*
*Volume I*, Palgrave Studies of Public Sector Management in Africa,
https://doi.org/10.1007/978-3-030-95394-2_7

Although corruption exists in all countries, it is more widespread in low-income countries (UNDP, 2008). This is not because people in poor countries are more corruptible than their counterparts in rich countries, it is simply because conditions in poor countries are more conducive for the growth of corruption (Justesen & Bjørnskov, 2014). Myint (2000) posits that corruption is most prevalent where there are other forms of institutional weaknesses, such as political instability, bureaucratic red tape, and weak legislative and judicial systems.

This chapter fundamentally seeks to examine the fight on corruption in public organisations in Africa and anti-corruption initiatives meant to address them. Essentially, it is an appraisal of established knowledge that seeks to unpack the fortes and faults of Africa's anti-corruption initiatives. It covers a broad spectrum of the African continent and untangles the causes and instances of corruption in public organisations. It seeks to explore the effect of corruption on the performance of public organisations from a holistic view.

# Corruption in Africa's Public Organisations: A Holistic Assessment

Corruption is a precarious cancer that eats deep into the ethical fibre of every organisation. The term "corruption" is often used to refer to unlawful activities carried out in any position of power. Although there is no universal definition of corruption, most definitions emphasise the misuse of public power or the use of a privileged position for personal gain. Because of the wide range of corruption patterns, assessing the current impact of anti-corruption measures has proven difficult. This is largely because corruption tendencies differ from society to society (Soreide, 2014; Hope, 2016). Several domestic and external underlying reasons have led to the emergence and spread of corruption in public organisations, according to the European Commission (2011). They include:

- The level of economic development and poverty in the country
- Unintended consequences of economic liberalisation policies

- Unintended consequences of State intervention programmes
- Incompetence of weak institutions
- Lack of accountability and transparency in public organisations
- Unintended consequences of international corporations' activities
- Negative effects of Foreign Direct Investment (FDI) on the local economy
- Tax havens and money laundering
- International organised crime

When corruption persists, it manifests itself as a systemic failure of governance and its primary institutions. Public institutions tasked with guaranteeing public accountability, adhering to ethics and integrity standards, and enforcing the rule of law get tainted and may become infested by corrupt individuals and syndicates. This creates a climate in which personal and communal impunity reigns supreme, and corruption becomes endemic (Hope, 1985; Gould, 2001; Sung, 2004).

In the business world, ethical considerations lie at the heart of public sector management. Fairness, justice, thoughtfulness, and social responsibility are at the forefront of the concerns in the day-to-day operations of these organisations. Public officials, for example, are seen as keepers of public trust and are therefore required to uphold the highest ethical and accountability standards. In other words, positive traits and attributes should lead their actions. However, the perpetual rise in reported examples of unethical behaviour, such as corruption and fraud, has increased public scrutiny of government actions.

There is a myriad of basic causes of corruption in Africa. Here, we try to highlight some of them in public organisations as experienced on the African continent.

## Culture of Corruption

Corrupt practices have become common in the running of public organisations. One main reason why corruption is so pervasive and why attempts to "combat" it are so difficult is because corruption has become such a powerful force multiplier in public administration. Those who participate in any type of corruption in their jobs have an advantage over those who do not. Bribes and kickbacks are not successfully penalised, and those who refuse to engage in the practice soon find themselves at a disadvantage politically and/or monetarily in comparison to their peers.

## Lack of Effective Leadership

Another issue that contributes to public sector corruption is a lack of adequate leadership to guide the organisation's operations. There are multiple examples of public sector officials who have run down enterprises they were expected to manage, as a result of their corruption behavior and practices. Like a virus, corruption can easily spread throughout an organisation. Shellukindo and Baguma (1993) present a vivid picture of the extent of this degeneration of ethics among African professionals when they point out that the situation is such that chief accountants have become "thief accountants" and managing directors have become "damaging directors."

## Personal Bias of Administrative Leaders

Owing to personal bias of administrative leaders, nepotism has become as rampant in public organisations as it is in our daily lives. Because of unscrupulous manoeuvres commonly referred to as "connections," many persons who do not have the requisite qualifications are found occupying positions in many top government organisations. It has become commonplace for Chief Executive Officers to hire family and clan members into key positions to promote their interests within the company. It is true that humans are intrinsically selfish and look out for their own interests, but the prevalence of such actions in the public sector is innately fuelled by the seeming endorsement of the political elite. It has become rather conventional for African leaders to appoint family members and relatives into political and administrative positions without any ethical apprehension of their actions. Such incidences thereby empower administrative leaders to do same, since those who put them into office have normalized it.

## Political Patronage

African politics can be regarded as corruption in action. The outcome of political actions has long been associated with corrupt practices, to the point where it has become ubiquitous on the African continent. Many countries are beset by the problem of ineffective government systems weakened by political corruption. This, in turn, has an impact on the performance of public organisations operating under the watchful eye of the government. Politicians have become accustomed to making a slew of promises to members of their political parties to earn political favour during elections, to court political favour and funding within the party. When they gain power, they are expected to repay these favours, either in cash or in kind.

## Harsh Economic Conditions

People who engage in corrupt behaviours are also influenced by difficult economic conditions. The consequent effect of harsh economic conditions for workers in the public sector means they tend to be more likely to accept bribes and engage in other illegal acts to supplement their generally low remuneration.

## Decline in Ethical Values

Africans' ethical ideals have likewise been steadily declining. This can be ascribed to a few issues, the most prominent of which being the "get-rich-quick" mentality that many people who work in public institutions have developed. Society has become consumed with vanity to the extent that the rich in society are seen as untouchable. Such perceptions are driven by the ever-increasing gap between the rich and the poor in society and the use of social media to constantly highlight the gulf in lifestyles. In some instances, even when the rich are indicted in corruption scandals, the manner with which their cases are handled and ignored reminds the ailing masses that corruption actually pays in this part of the world. As such, it has become normal to see colleagues who are on the same low salaries, living large with impunity. This has subsequently created a culture of ethical misconduct and a proliferation of corrupt practices in the public sector.

## Heavy Social Dependency Structures

Corruption equally thrives in African societies because of the heavy social dependency nature of the communities. The structure of a typical African society promotes social reliance and hails those who can display wealth and provide financial care for their community. This puts pressure on people to cut corners, to support the members of their communities. Such a perception is usually coupled with the impression that working for the government brings with it a high level of financial remuneration. The corruption of others in this sector who have inexplicable sources of wealth appears to create a narrative that individuals who work in public organisations are wealthy enough to absorb the troubles of many in their communities.

# Anti-corruption Instruments

## African Union Convention on Preventing and Combating Corruption (AUCPCC)

The African Union Convention on Preventing and Combating Corruption (AUCPCC) was adopted on 11 July 2003 to combat widespread corruption on the continent. As of 1 January 2020, the treaty had been ratified by 43 out of the 49 States which signed it. By ratifying the AUCPCC, all State Parties are expected to domesticate their national legislative and policy instruments aimed at combating corruption. The convention represents what African countries should do in terms of asset recovery, criminality, international collaboration, and prevention. The AUCPCC calls for the eradication of corruption in the private and public sectors (Olajide, 2014). Bribery (domestic or international), diversion of property by public officials, trafficking in influence, illicit enrichment, money laundering, and concealment of property are all covered under the Convention, which principally comprises mandatory clauses. It also requires the States which have signed the agreement to conduct open and transparent investigations into corruption in their home countries.

The Convention outlines some specific guidelines that African States are expected to implement to combat corruption and related offences in the public service. African States are required to commit themselves to the following provisions of Article 7:

- Require all public officials to declare their assets during and after the time of assuming office in the public service.
- Create an internal committee or a similar body mandated to establish a code of conduct and to monitor its implementation and sensitise and train public officials on matters of ethics.
- Develop disciplinary measures and investigation procedures in corruption and related offences, with a view to keeping up with technology and increase the efficiency of those responsible in this regard.
- Ensure transparency, equity, and efficiency in the management of tendering and hiring procedures in public organisations.
- Subject to the provisions of domestic legislation, any immunity granted to public officials shall not be an obstacle to the investigation of allegations against and the prosecution of such officials.

Unfortunately, the AU Convention does not make it mandatory for States to adopt some of the necessary anti-corruption measures. It simply requires them to "commit themselves" to having all public officials declare their assets when they begin their terms of office, during, and after tenures in the public service.

For Member States to implement the provisions as stipulated in the Convention, there need to be targets set for these countries to achieve with a stipulated timeframe to encourage compliance. Eighteen years after, the treaty seems to be long forgotten. It is impossible to track the progress which has been made, what impact the treaty has had on members, and if they even abide by it. When in 2018, the African Union declared the year as the Year for Anti-corruption under the theme "Winning the Fight Against Corruption: A Sustainable Path to Africa's Transformation," not even one African country released a statement to commemorate the day or to provide an update on the progress that had been made with the AUCPCC protocol. Contrary to the glamorous theme indicated in the 2018 event, Africa is not winning the fight against corruption.

## United Nations Convention Against Corruption (UNCAC)

The United Nations Convention Against Corruption (UNCAC) is a landmark, international anti-corruption treaty adopted by the UN General Assembly in October 2003. It is the only legally binding universal anti-corruption instrument. UNCAC has so far binded 187 countries (as of May 2020), making it unusual not only in its global reach but also in the breadth of its provisions, which recognise the necessity of both preventive and punitive measures. It also tackles the worldwide aspect of corruption by including measures on international collaboration and the return of corrupt proceeds. States that have ratified the Convention are also required to provide technical assistance to one another. The Convention also emphasises the significance of citizens' access to information and advocates for the participation of the public and civil society accountability processes.

Article 6(2) of UNCAC mandates the creation of institutions to address the threat of corruption and states: "Each State Party shall ensure the existence of a body or bodies, as appropriate, which prevents corruption." Each State Party shall provide these bodies with the necessary independence, consistent with the fundamental principles of its legal systems, to allow them to carry out their functions efficiently and without undue influence. The required material resources and specialised personnel, as well as the training that such personnel requires to perform their duties, should be provided. Article 6(2) does not directly indicate that countries should have a single anti-corruption agency; rather, it states that countries should "enable the body or bodies to carry out its or their function," as well as "ensure the existence of a body or bodies." However, Holmes (2015) suggests that instead of various anti-corruption bodies, a single independent anti-corruption agency be established, as this is an institutional change that can be implemented across countries with diverse cultures.

# Similarities Between the AUCPCC and the UNCAC

There are three points that the AUCPCC and the UNCAC have in common. To begin with, they both suggest that combating corruption is a team effort involving governments in both developed and developing countries, the private sector, organisations, and individuals.

Second, because corruption is harmful to political and socio-economic progress, it must be prevented or combated by reforms, improved systems and processes, and the use of punishments.

Third, these instruments raise the fight against corruption high at both national and international levels and encourage anti-corruption dialogue to implement all the anti-corruption legal frameworks.

## Anti-corruption Ecosystems

Fighting corruption in the public sector today is not only confined to the State and public agencies. Non-State and civil society bodies are also active in corruption control. Although each country must develop and drive its own national responses to corruption, it is now widely accepted that in a globalised world, international cooperation to address corruption is vital. Therefore, the fight has taken a more inclusive approach with organisations engaging various other stakeholders to contribute to national anti-corruption efforts. Below is an illustration of what a typical anti-corruption ecosystem looks like (Fig. 7.1).

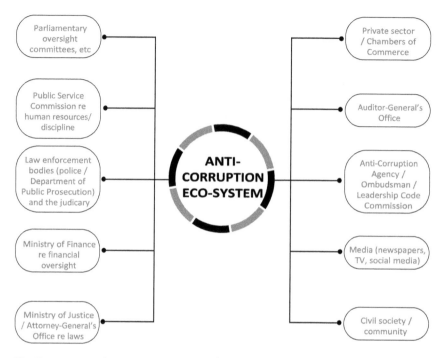

Fig. 7.1  A typical anti-corruption ecosystem. (Source: UNODC, 2020)

There are already some agencies in national set-ups such as ministries, public service commissions, and parliamentary committees that are supposed to ensure that corrupt activities never arise. However, with the support from civil society groups, the media, and other non-state actors, the fight is becoming less biased and effectual. Thanks to the expansion of media freedom, relaxation of censorship, and overall liberalisation of the media environment, an independent media with a zeal for investigating and exposing official wrongdoing has emerged.

Furthermore, the development of associational freedoms in the new age has produced the emergence of civil society organisations, including anti-corruption non-governmental organisations such as Transparency International (TI) national chapters and other citizen watchdog groups.

The efforts of key non-state organisations such as the International Monetary Fund (IMF), the World Bank, and the Organisation for Economic Co-operation and Development (OECD) cannot be understated. For instance, the IMF (2016) proposed four critical strategies to combat public sector corruption. They include transparency, rule of law, economic reform strategies aimed at reducing excessive regulation, and effective institutions, which include the creation of a competitive public service that prides itself on being free of both corporate and public influence. Such inputs go on to strengthen the anti-corruption ecosystem and serve as guide in shaping the thoughts and decision-making processes of all countries.

# Regional Anti-corruption Initiatives

## Evidence from Southern Africa

### The Southern African Development Community (SADC) Protocol Against Corruption

The Southern African Development Community (SADC) is a Regional Economic Community in Southern Africa made up of 16 countries that, among other things, support the region's development agenda. The SADC was formed in August 1992, and it is the first sub-regional treaty to fight corruption in Africa. The signatory-countries include Angola, Botswana, Comoros, Democratic Republic of Congo, Eswatini, Lesotho, Madagascar, Malawi, Mauritius, Mozambique, Namibia, Seychelles, South Africa, Tanzania, Zambia, and Zimbabwe. They formed the SADC Protocol Against Corruption in 2005 as part of their accord to combat corruption issues in the region.

The Protocol calls for the development of standards of conduct for public officials as one of the measures. One code of ethics prohibits public officials from using their positions to obtain private presents or other benefits for themselves while carrying out their official obligations. The significance of such a norm is that it helps to keep officials on track by continuously stirring their conscience.

The Protocol also proposes the creation of "permanent institutions charged with implementing measures for preventing, detecting, punishing, and eliminating bribery and corruption." The Protocol clearly calls for specialised institutions in addition to conventional police or law enforcement authorities, based on the tone of the clause. To be effective, these anti-corruption institutions must be independent of the executive branch of government, have the authority to launch investigations and prosecute individuals, and have the political support of the powers-that-be.

The Protocol also requires that the hire of personnel and procurement of goods and services must be transparent, equitable, and efficient. To meet the requirements of transparency, equity, and efficiency, the hiring systems must be open: the positions to be filled as well as the required qualifications must be advertised as widely as possible; the selection procedures to be followed must be accessible to all prospective candidates and must be applied fairly and uniformly to all of them; where interviews are considered necessary, they must be conducted fairly and by disinterested and impartial individuals.

The Protocol requires State Parties to establish systems that deter corruption and to enact laws that deny favourable tax treatment to any individual or corporation for expenditures made for corrupt purposes. It also requires states to maintain and strengthen mechanisms that promote access to information. It is believed that easy access to such information by ventilating governmental operations helps in eradicating or eliminating opportunities for corruption.

Since its inception, the Protocol has been able to maintain peace and stability in the region, contributed towards political stability, promoting solidarity among Member States, aided in the establishment of a free trade area which has ultimately led to an increase in intra-regional trade. Solidarity among Member States has been highlighted as being key in spearheading efforts that ultimately resulted in Namibia's attainment of independence in 1990 and the end of apartheid in South Africa in 1994.

In the fight against corruption, the SADC hosts an annual SADC anti-corruption sub-committee meeting to reflect on the progress that has been made on anti-corruption initiatives, as well as the implementation of the SADC Protocol Against Corruption. The sub-committee set out an SADC anti-corruption action plan for 2018–2022, which sought to foster regional collaboration against corruption. Fast forward 2021, it is unclear what the targets of the action plan are, if they have been met, and how these action plans would contribute to the broader protocol in the fight against corruption.

## Evidence from Eastern Africa

### The East African Community (EAC) Draft Protocol on Preventing and Combating Corruption

The East African Community (EAC) is a regional intergovernmental organisation founded in July 2000 under Article 2 of the Treaty for the Establishment of the East African Community. The membership of the Community comprises the Republics of Burundi, Kenya, Rwanda, Uganda, and the United Republic of Tanzania. In 2010, countries that make up this community were hoping to finalise a regional protocol to fight corruption and create anti-corruption initiatives for the community. The bone of contention was the role of local anti-corruption agencies in exerting their prosecutorial powers on cases. The inability of these countries to agree on a final arrangement has meant that the protocol remains in draft form.

## Evidence from Western Africa

### Economic Community of West African States (ECOWAS) Protocol on the Fight Against Corruption

The Economic Community of West African States Protocol on the Fight Against Corruption is an anti-corruption initiative by the Heads of State and Government of the Member States of the Economic Community of West African States (ECOWAS).

The objectives of the Protocol are to promote and strengthen the development in each of the State Parties effective mechanisms to prevent, suppress, and eradicate corruption; to intensify and revitalise cooperation between State Parties, with a view to making anti-corruption measures more effective; and to promote the harmonisation and coordination of national anti-corruption laws and policies.

Evidence suggests that this Protocol has not achieved as much as it ought to with the rising cases of corruption in the sub-region a key indicator. The region's major economies—Nigeria, Cote d'Ivoire, Ghana, and Senegal—continue to under-perform, with flat or declining scores in Transparency International's Corruption Index, with Ghana being tagged as "the country to watch" because of its continuous steady decline on the rankings. To improve upon things, countries need to develop the political will and establish measures in to actually implement the provisions of the Protocol they have signed.

## Evidence from Northern Africa

### The MENA-OECD Initiative

The Middle East and North Africa (MENA)-OECD Initiative was created in 2005 to bring together the Middle East and North Africa to collaborate on issues of economic development, trade, and tackling corruption in the region. Member Countries comprise Algeria, Bahrain, Djibouti, Egypt, Iraq, Jordan, Kuwait, Lebanon, Libya, Mauritania, Morocco, Oman, Palestinian Authority, Qatar, Saudi Arabia, Syria, Tunisia, United Arab Emirates, and Yemen.

The initiative is carried out in partnership with the United Nations Convention Against Corruption (UNCAC), which represents the only legally binding universal anti-corruption instrument and covers many different forms of corruption such as bribery, trading in influence, abuse of functions, and various acts of corruption in the private sector.

The initiative has been so far successful in initiating other programmes such as the MENA-OECD competitiveness programme that supports reforms to mobilise investment, private sector development, and entrepreneurship as driving forces for inclusive growth and employment in the MENA region, and the MENA-OECD governance programme that supports public sector reforms in view of unlocking social and economic development and of meeting citizens' growing expectations on quality services, inclusive policymaking, and transparency.

However, it is problematic to measure the impacts that this initiative has had on the fight against corruption in the sub-region. The initiative neither explicitly provides any outline as to how it seeks to combat corruption in the sub-region nor provides any information on the progress made so far or the challenges faced.

## Evidence from Central Africa

Countries in Central Africa generally have membership in most of the anti-corruption conventions and treaties highlighted above. Regional treaties such as the Economic Community of Central African States (ECCAS), the International Conference on the Great Lakes Region, and Central Africa Economic and Monetary Community are examples of stakeholder engagements involving Central African countries on issues of peace and security, trade, and economic stability. There are explicitly no formal protocols on anti-corruption in the region. Aside from the meeting of the African Organisation of English-Speaking Supreme Audit Institutions (AFROSAI-E), which tackles corruption in the public sector and comprises Central African States, there are essentially no other stakeholder engagements on anti-corruption on a regional level. This may be due to the increased threat of insecurity in those regions, being the topmost priority in their regional agenda. Other factors such as the political fragility in the region and the plethora of military regimes in that region could also account for why anti-corruption issues do not form premium content on their regional menu.

### African Organisation of English-Speaking Supreme Audit Institutions (AFROSAI-E)

AFROSAI was founded in 2005 with the goal of promoting and enhancing shared ideas and experiences among Africa's supreme audit institutions on public finance auditing. These institutions play an important role in national accountability and audits, and they hold governments accountable for the use of public funds. Countries such as Rwanda and Cameroon in the Central African region are key members of this group.

As part of their anti-corruption efforts, AFROSAI in 2018 conducted a "coordinated compliance and performance audit on corruption as a driver of IFFs" (AFROSAI, 2018: 4). The auditors investigated the extent to which 12 African nations implemented the UNCAC and the AUCPCC, focusing on asset disclosures and public procurement procedures.

The audit showed a lack of uniform regulatory framework on asset disclosures because of significant country differences. It therefore recommended countries to apply meaningful consequences for non-compliance, as well as improved declaration verification and public access to declarations. It supported competitive and effective procurement procedures, improved management of conflicts of interest, asset disclosures by procurement authorities, and strengthened procurement supervision.

## A Mini Case Study of Ghana

In recent years, the subject of corruption, particularly how to manage it, has resurfaced as a major issue in the Ghanaian anti-corruption conversation. To a larger context, anti-corruption rhetoric and programmes seem to exist in name rather than in reality. This high incidence and perception of corruption led to the formulation of the National Anti-corruption Action Plan (NACAP), from 2015 to 2024 (Republic of Ghana, 2011). The vision of the NACAP is to create a sustainable democratic society founded on good governance and imbued with high ethics and integrity. Its mission is to contextualise and mobilise efforts and resources of stakeholders, including government, individuals, civil society, private sector, and the media, to prevent and fight corruption through the promotion of high ethics and integrity and the vigorous enforcement of applicable laws.

NACAP's vision, purpose, and strategic objectives emphasise several points. First, they demonstrate sensitivity to the political objectives of the Directive Principles of State Policy, particularly those relating to the establishment of a democratic state to promote freedom, justice, and fundamental human rights and freedoms, as well as the implementation of measures to eliminate corruption and the abuse of power. Second, the scope of NACAP extends beyond regulating corruption in the public sector to private, state, and non-state actors of all genders, ages, local and international standing, and so does not point accusing fingers at any one sector for corruption in Ghana. Third, there is the desire to develop a long-term anti-corruption culture among Ghanaians through prevention, proactive, sustained and coordinated education, and investigation and sanctions. Fourth, there is a focus on enhanced investigation and punishment of criminals, as well as appropriate funding for 13 anti-corruption agencies.

There have also been some interventions by successive Ghanaian governments to contribute to its anti-corruption initiatives. Some of these processes are outlined below:

| Interventions to combat corruption in Ghana's public sector | |
|---|---|
| Administrative Reforms | Public sector reforms; Civil Service Reform Programme, 1987–1993; National Institutional Renewal Programme, 1994; the Civil Service Performance Improvement Programme, 1995 to date; privatisation of state enterprises; Public Sector Management Reform Programme from 1997 to date; legal sector reform; Public Financial Management Reform Programme (PUFMARP) and decentralisation and local government; National Governance Programme; and Ghana Integrated Financial Management Information Systems (GIFMIS). |
| Institutional Reforms | People's Defence Committees and Workers Defence Committees (WDCs) under the PNDC government and renamed Committees for the Defence of the Revolution (CDRs); Citizens Vetting Committee established in 1982 and renamed Office of Revenue Commissioners in 1984; National Investigation Committee established in 1982; Bureau of National Investigations (BNI); Economic Crime Unit of the Police Service; Commission on Human Rights and Administrative Justice (CHRAJ); Auditor-General and Serious Fraud Office (SFO), all created in 1993; SFO is renamed Economic and Organised Crime Office (2010); Auditor General; Public Accounts Committee of Parliament; Financial Intelligence Centre. |

Source: Adopted from Ayee (2016)

There are also anti-corruption bodies (both state and non-state) including the Commission on Human Rights and Administrative Justice (CHRAJ) (1993), the Economic and Organised Crime Office (EOCO) (2010), the Financial Intelligence Centre (2010), the Ghana Integrity Initiative (2010; the local chapter of Transparency International), and the Ghana Anti-Corruption Coalition that have spearheaded the anti-corruption fight in the public sector. Nonetheless, they have encountered roadblocks in their anti-corruption quest, because of the enormous, pervasive, and systemic nature of corruption, which requires a multi-dimensional, multi-pronged, and multi-agency response (Ayee, 2016).

# Recommendations

There is the need for a comprehensive and systemic strategy that provides the much-needed solution to the issue of corruption, starting from the local level. Countries need to endeavour to keep their house in order before they can realistically attempt to alter the current status quo on a regional or continental level. To achieve this, there are some recommendations on what African countries can do at both the local and continental levels.

To begin, political parties should be made to disclose the source of funding for political activities. As highlighted in the early junctures of this chapter, the driving force behind corrupt practices vastly includes the need to reciprocate political favours that were made to political elite, especially during the season of political campaigns and elections. It is conventional in many African countries for political parties and candidates to contest an election without declaring their assets or sources of funding. This leaves room for malice and creates a system where politicians and political parties are funded from inexplicable sources. As a result, when these politicians come into power, they are obliged to pay back these favours by appointing these financiers and bankrollers into top government and administrative positions. Those who do not receive political appointments are awarded contracts through rigged processes. This is not to say once politicians and political parties are made to declare their assets, corruption will cease. However, such transparent measures will help to reduce the tendencies of corruption. Public auditing of persons who are vying to take up political position will also help dispel false notions that all public servants are thieves. This is the only way our political leaders can be held more accountable, and the urge to reciprocate political favours will vastly reduce, while appeasing the general public.

In continuation, there is a need for the enforcement of existing anti-corruption laws. In many African countries, there are more than enough laws to locally address corrupt practices. Several commissions have been established to generate anti-corruption reforms, to help implement the provisions of the continental and regional agreements. Yet, the results of these initiatives are not evident, and corruption continues to flourish. To address this, countries should put in more efforts in enforcing existing anti-corruption laws. Clear targets should be set, and there should be an unblemished pathway to achieving their objectives. There should be political will to enforce provisions of signed conventions and treaties because that is the only way the fight against corruption can truly be effective.

Furthermore, States must also establish measures to properly investigate, prosecute, and legally sanction all reported cases of corruption, with no exception. It is routine in Africa to have top administrative officials and the political elites indicted for corrupt practices, only for them to be exonerated. It is increasingly rare to see governments prosecuting members of their administrations for corrupt crimes committed during their tenure in office. Usually, what happens in such cases of corruption is probed only when an opposition party effectively comes into power. The downside with this also is that once the opposition begins to probe, they are tagged as pursuing a political vendetta against the previous government, and thus, the cycle continues. The way forward will be to develop a culture and ethos of integrity, transparency, and accountability in the institutions that have been created to help to fight corruption, so that they can carry out their duties efficiently without any external interferences from political actors.

Finally, there should be training and education of public administrators in ethics and ethical behaviour. African countries should invest more in the training of their public officials and administrators on the dos and don'ts in public service administration. These training programmes should adopt a bottom-up approach and should not only focus on officials who lead these organisations but should trickle down and target those at the bottom of the organisational hierarchy. This way, they will become abreast with the ethical requirements of public administration and acquire traits that they are more likely to replicate when they get to the top.

## Conclusion

Corruption has been prevalent for a significant period in Africa. This has created genuine dilemma for agencies and policymakers engaged in anti-corruption campaigns and public sector reforms in Africa. Judging by the number of programmes currently being implemented across the continent, it is obvious that the will to combat corruption has become more robust, and this has created a renewed sense of hope for a corrupt-free Africa in the future. The war against corruption in Africa is however far from over. Progress has been made, but African states would need to do more to implement the plethora of conventions that they have currently assented to. Heads of public organisations and institutions will also need to take bold steps to tackle the issues within their organisations. Current indications however suggests that although the conventions have been signed on paper, the political will to execute them by the signatories is scant.

## References

AFROSAI, (2018). Integrated annual report. See: https://afrosaie.org.za/2018/05/21/integrated-annual-report-2018/

Ayee, J. (2016). *Anti-corruption measures in Ghana: An analysis of the National Anti-Corruption Action Plan* (Ghana policy dialogue series). African Development Bank.

Gould, D. J. (2001). Administrative Corruption: Incidence, Causes, and Remedial Strategies. In A. Farazmand (ed.), *Handbook of Comparative and Development Public Administration* (2nd ed). New York: Marcel Dekker.

Holmes, L. (2015). *Corruption: A very short introduction*. Oxford University Press.

Hope, K. R. (1985). Politics, Bureaucratic Corruption, and Maladministration in the Third World. *International Review of Administrative Sciences, 51*(1), 1–6.

Hope, K. R. (2016). The corruption problem in Swaziland: Consequences and some aspects of policy to combat it. *Journal of Developing Societies, 32*(2), 130–158.

International Monetary Fund. (2016). *Corruption: Costs and mitigating strategies*. IMF Discussion Note SDN/16/05 May.

Justesen, M. K., & Bjørnskov, C. (2014). Exploiting the poor: Bureaucratic corruption and Poverty in Africa. *World Development, 58*, 106–115.

Lambsdorff, J. G. (2007). *The institutional economics of corruption and reform: Theory, evidence and policy*. Cambridge University Press.

Myint, U. (2000). Corruption: Causes, consequences and cures. *Asia-Pacific Development Journal, 7*(2), 33–58.

Olajide, B. A. (2014). United Nations and African Union Conventions on Corruption and Anti-corruption Legislations in Nigeria: A Comparative Analysis. *African Journal of International & Comparative Law, 22*(2), 308–333. https://doi.org/10.3366/ajicl.2014.0094. ISSN 0954-8890.

Republic of Ghana. (2011). *National Anti-Corruption Action Plan (2015–2024)*. Government Printer.

Rose-Ackerman, S., & Soreide, T. (2011). *The international handbook on the economics of corruption* (Vol. 2). Edward Elgar Publishing.

Shellukindo, W. N., & Baguma, R. (1993). Ethical standards and behaviour in African public services. In S. Rasheed & D. Olowu (Eds.), *Ethics and accountability in African public services*. African Association for Public Administration and Management (AAPAM).

Soreide, T. (2014). *Drivers of corruption: A brief review*. World Bank.

Sung, H. E. (2004). Democracy and Political Corruption: A Cross-National Comparison. *Crime, Law and Social Change, 41*(2004), 179–194.

United Nations Development Program. (2008). *Tackling corruption, transforming lives: Accelerating human development in Asia and the Pacific*. United Nations Development Program, 2008.

United Nations Economic Commission for Africa. (2011). *Combating corruption, improving governance in Africa regional anti-corruption programme for Africa (2011–2016)*. UNECA.

United Nations Office on Drugs and Crimes. (2020). Corruption and economic crime branch [online]. https://www.unodc.org/unodc/en/corruption/about.html

World Bank. (2015). *World development report: Mind, society and behavior.* World Bank.

# 8

# Public Service Performance Management

Arinze Nwokolo

## Introduction

Effective functioning of public service is important for economic growth and poverty reduction, especially in Sub-Saharan Africa. Performance management and appraisal matter for the effective functioning of public service bureaucracies. A central question in public administration is the relationship between the managerial practices of public servants (performance management) and organisational performance (appraisal) (Ingraham, 2007; Lynn et al., 2000). It is also an issue of debate. According to Miller and Whitford (2016), this debate is between two broad schools of thought, namely, those that support incentives and monitoring of bureaucrats,[1] following Herman Finer (Finer, 1941) and

---

[1] A bureaucrat is an official in a government ministry (public sector) who is perceived to be concerned with procedural correctness at the expense of people's needs.

---

A. Nwokolo (✉)
Lagos Business School, Pan-Atlantic University, Lagos, Nigeria
e-mail: anwokolo@lbs.edu.ng

© The Author(s), under exclusive license to Springer Nature Switzerland AG 2022    **153**
K. Ogunyemi et al. (eds.), *Ethics and Accountable Governance in Africa's Public Sector,*
*Volume I*, Palgrave Studies of Public Sector Management in Africa,
https://doi.org/10.1007/978-3-030-95394-2_8

supporters of autonomy and discretion to bureaucrats, following Carl Friedrich (Friedrich, 1978). On the one hand, the management practice of incentive provision and monitoring is based on the principle that, given the divergence of bureaucrats' preferences from those of the public good, it is necessary to manage them through top-down tools of control such as monitoring, rewards and sanctions, to elicit effort from bureaucrats in the performance of their duties. In other words, the incentives/ monitoring management practice captures the extent to which indicators of project performance are gathered, reviewed and used to reward bureaucrats. Theoretically, it posits that performance incentives and monitoring have a positive impact on organisational performance and should be rewarded through a performance-related pay (PRP) scheme. However, certain features of the public sector make uncertain the impact of incentives such as multiple principals (the action of one government bureaucracy or service agency produce externalities), multiple tasks (most public agencies perform several tasks and sometimes do not have a clear objective), lack of competition (most government agencies are monopolies), motivating agents (intrinsic motivation of public service agents may be crowded out by performance incentives). On the other hand, the management practice of autonomy and discretion perceive bureaucrats as professionals who do their best for the public good through their expertise. Hence, public bureaucracies should delegate more autonomy and discretion to bureaucrats for this reason. In theory, this management practice captures the degree to which bureaucrats contribute to policy formulation and (bottom-up) policy implementation processes and how they can easily be reorganised to respond to best practices and project peculiarities. It also encompasses other theoretical views in the public administration literature: from the view that bureaucrats should be assigned decision-making roles and given the freedom to rely on their professionalism to deliver public services, to the perspective that the divergence between the objectives of society and bureaucracy necessitates a rule-based system of public administration to ensure acceptable and consistent levels of public service delivery.

# Performance-Related Pay and Public Service Performance Management

Performance-related pay scheme is a compensation arrangement whereby an employee's final salary is a function of a measured "performance" in which who measures it and the variation of the performance measure and its link to salary are key design aspects of the scheme (Hasnain et al., 2012). Hence, it can be based on qualitative assessments or quantitative measures of inputs, outputs or outcomes. Salary, as a function of performance can be at a piece-rate pay, commission-based or a combination of base pay and one-off bonuses or merits. Evaluations are made by direct supervisors or human resource specialists in the organisation.

The relationship between public service performance and the use of incentives and monitoring is theoretically unclear. This is because of the mismatch between the nature of public sector workers and the practicality of incentives and monitoring practice. The management practice of incentives and monitoring elicits the bureaucrats' effort and discourages behaviour misaligned with the preferences of the public sector. However, public sector work involves multiple goals, hard-to-measure outcomes and outputs, considerable coordination and environmental uncertainty that limit the practice of incentives and monitoring or cause it to backfire (Rasul et al., 2021). To address this challenge, the performance-related pay (PRP) scheme was introduced as a tool to improve public sector productivity and accountability. However, there are mixed results of success and failure regarding the effect of PRP on public sector performance. According to the literature on public administration, there are three explanations for this (Bellé, 2015). First is the inability of the performance management systems that support incentive systems and the lack of technical design of contingent pay plans. In other words, performance-related pay practices will be effective if they are better designed and supported by better performance management practices (e.g., performance appraisal systems), which are often lacking in public sector organisations (Marsden & Richardson, 1994; Moynihan et al., 2011). Second, the fundamental institutional characteristics of organisations in the public sector cannot be adjusted through improving performance management practices. Such characteristics include transparency requirements regarding compensation policies (Colella et al., 2007), budget constraints and public expectations on the responsible stewardship of resources which make it impossible for public workers to receive bonuses that are large enough to be effective (Miller & Whitford, 2006). However, incentives are likely to be effective in administrations in which there is a relative separation between the beneficiaries of the incentives (e.g., politicians) and the managers of the incentive system (e.g., senior civil servants). Incentives will be less credible and less likely to be effective if the interests of both groups overlap (Dahlstrom & Lapuente, 2010). Third, the motivational differences between the public sector and private sector employees are another drawback of PRP in the public sector organisation. On the one hand, financial incentives are more likely to crowd out intrinsic motivation in public organisations. In other words, given that financial incentives produce two opposing effects by increasing extrinsic motivation (price effect) and crowding out[2] intrinsic motivations of individuals (crowding-out effect) by intimidating their feeling of autonomy and competence. The overall impact of incentive on PRP is likely to be weaker in the public sector since, compared to the private sector, since incentives are usually smaller in the public sector. This implies that incentives will have little effect on the extrinsic motivation and a large effect on the intrinsic motivation of public sector employees because they are more intrinsically motivated than private sector employees (Weibel et al., 2010). On the other hand, financial incentives may weaken the motivations of public employees by crowding out image motivation (i.e., the tendency to be motivated by "the desire to be liked and respected by others and by one's self"). Hence, performance-related pay (PRP) will have a larger effect on performance of public employees if rewards are undisclosed rather than when they are disclosed (Bellé, 2015).

---

[2] Crowding out effect is an economic theory which argues that an increase in public sector spending reduces or even eliminates spending in the private sector.

# Public Service Motivation and Corruption

As mentioned earlier, the public management practice of giving auton-omy and discretion to public employees is based on the belief that bureau-crats possess the skill to do good for others and society. Yet, studies show this practice has a potential downside such as corruption (Kwon, 2014; Olken & Pande, 2012) and also a positive effect on policy implementa-tion by bureaucrats (Rasul & Rogger, 2018; Thomann et al., 2018). Corruption is prevalent at all tiers of government bureaucracy in Africa and is typically considered a major obstacle to economic development. A suggested solution to this is the promotion of management practices through activating bureaucrats' public service motivation (PSM) to chan-nel their service delivery for the good of the public and society. This motivation may help public managers to engage in making ethical deci-sions. PSM comprises four components: self-sacrifice, commitment to public values, attraction to public service, and compassion. Each compo-nent affects ethical behaviour through ethical intent which promotes the willingness of public servants to report ethical problems to management. Self-sacrifice portrays the willingness to sacrifice one's interest for the greater good (Wright et al., 2016). A commitment to public values com-prises values embedded in one's internal moral compass that is grounded in personal integrity reflection and virtue (Stazyk & Davis, 2015). Individuals who are attracted to public service and value it, usually view tackling social problems as their primary reward. This helps them to engage in prosocial and ethical behaviour (Brewer & Selden, 1998). Lastly, compassion can curb unethical behaviour through altruism and sympathy for the welfare of others (DeSteno, 2015). Empirical results show that PSM activation enhances the willingness, of public employees, to report ethical problems to management (Meyer-Sahling et al., 2019). It also increases performance and integrity in the public sector (Bellé, 2014; Kwon, 2014). In addition, PSM is a good predictor of corruption and altruism. High levels of PSM are associated with a low propensity to engage in corruption and high levels of altruistic behaviour (Gans-Morse et al., 2021).

# New Public Management, Digital Era Governance and Civil Reforms

The New Public Management (NPM) approach took place, during the 1980s, in the context of civil reforms in the United States, Great Britain, Canada, Australia, New Zealand and continental Europe (Pollitt & Bouckaert, 2011). This approach was based on the hypothesis that the adoption of private sector management style and market-oriented approach in the public sector will improve cost-efficiency and quality. Hence, it emphasised giving authority and autonomy to bureaucrats. It also involved the delegation of duties by governments to smaller agencies as well as providing frameworks that encourage competition between the public and private sectors and between different parts of the public sector (Dunleavy et al., 2005). In other words, NPM was based on the assumption that the public sector can be improved by importing business concepts, techniques and values from the private sector such as greater emphasis on output measurement and performance targets, smaller organisations, use of contracts and treating service users as customers (Fishenden & Thompson, 2013). NPM can also be viewed as a two-level phenomenon (Dunleavy, 1994). First, as a theory of managerial change, it is based on concepts imported from modern business practices and public choice—influenced theory into the public sector. Second, the changes in NPM were driven by the application of economic, business, and public choice ideas to practical problems in public sector provision.

These concepts from modern business practices revolve around three integral themes: Disaggregation, Competition and Incentivisation (Dunleavy et al., 2005). Disaggregation involves dividing large public sector hierarchies into flexible multi-firm structures and using management information systems to sustain them. The theme of Competition entails creating purchaser and supplier separation in public structures and encouraging more competition among potential suppliers of services. Incentivisation theme implies rewarding performance in the public sector through pecuniary-based, specific performance incentives. The components of themes are shown below in Table 8.1.

**Table 8.1** The key components of new public management (NPM)

| Theme | Components |
|---|---|
| Disaggregation | Purchaser-provider separation |
| | Agencification |
| | Decoupling policy systems |
| | Growth of quasi-government agencies |
| | Separation of micro-local agencies |
| | Chunking up privatised industries |
| | Corporatisation and strong single |
| | Organisation management |
| | De-professionalisation |
| | Competition by comparison |
| | Improved performance measurement |
| | League tables of agency performance |
| Competition | Quasi-markets |
| | Voucher schemes |
| | Outsourcing |
| | Compulsory market testing |
| | Intra-government contracting |
| | Public/private sectoral polarisation |
| | Product market liberalisation |
| | Deregulation |
| | Consumer-tagged financing |
| | User control |
| Incentivisation | Re-specifying property rights |
| | Light touch regulation |
| | Capital market involvement in projects |
| | Privatising asset ownership |
| | Anti-rent-seeking measures |
| | De-privileging professions |
| | Performance-related pay |
| | PFI (private finance initiative) |
| | Public-private partnerships |
| | Unified rate of return and discounting |
| | Development of charging technologies |
| | Valuing public sector equity |
| | Mandatory efficiency dividends |

Source: Summarised and adapted from Dunleavy et al. (2005)

The NPM policy regime increased institutional and policy complexity. Its focus on disaggregation and competition increased the number of administrative units and created more complex interrelationships among them. Besides, it made it more difficult for citizens to understand internal state arrangements. The failure of NPM to achieve its promised benefits led governments to move away from NPM to Digital Era Governance (DEG). DEG is characterised by public service re-aggregation under direct government control around the citizen and other technological changes inside the government as a response to the recent digital phenomena moving advanced industrial societies further towards an online civilisation (Margetts & Dunleavy, 2013). It can be explained in terms of three identifiable strategic themes: reintegration, holism and digitisation. Reintegration comprises rolling back the creation of semi-autonomous agencies, procurement concentration, reintegrating outsourcing and shared services. Holism encapsulates reorganising services around the citizen. It includes a one-stop service provider that is supported by data warehousing and evaluation of services based on the notions of the social web. Digitisation includes using online channel strategies to digitally deliver services through automated processes, open information and data, cloud and web services. An important characteristic of DEG is that its features are deeply innovative in the sense that they rely on both the emergence of new technologies and on new business models and supporting commercial incentives (Fishenden & Thompson, 2013). The innovative features of DEG are summarised in Table 8.2 below:

# Management Practices of Bureaucrats in African Countries Such as Nigeria, Ghana, and Uganda

This section describes studies on public service performance management practices in the Nigerian, Ghanaian and Ugandan civil service. It considers whether management practices matter for public service and how it correlates with the delivery of public projects and performance management.

# Nigeria

The study by Rasul and Rogger (2018) considers the correlates of effective public service delivery in Nigeria. It combined novel data sources that linked outputs of government bureaucracies with survey data that

**Table 8.2**  Innovative features of DEG

| DEG theme | Innovative feature |
| --- | --- |
| Reintegration | Network simplification |
| | Single tax and benefit systems using real-time data |
| | Decentralised delivery |
| | Radical disintermediation in public service-delivery chains |
| | Delivery-level joined-up governance |
| Holism | Interactive and "ask once" information-seeking and provision |
| | Agile processes (e.g., exceptions handling, real-time forecasting and preparedness) |
| | Joined-up delivery of local public services |
| | Co-production of services |
| | Online reputational evaluations in public services, including citizens' testimonials and open book government |
| | Development of "social web" processes and field services |
| | Single benefits integration in welfare states |
| | Single citizen account |
| | Integrated service shops at the central/federal level |
| | New service-delivery models linked to austerity and central disengagement |
| Digitisation | Active channel streaming, customer segmentation |
| | "100% online" channel strategies and mandated channel reductions (potential removal in part or whole of government agencies and departments) "government cloud" and government apps |
| | Free storage and data retention |
| | Web-based utility computing |
| | New forms of automated processes (e.g., zero-touch) |
| | Isocratic administration (e.g., coproduction of services) |
| | "Rich" technology-driven by "social web" |
| | Freeing public information for reuse, mash-ups, and so on. |

Evidence from the five sub-regions of Africa (North, East, Central, West, and Southern)
Source: Adapted from Fishenden and Thompson (2013)

elicits a range of management practices that bureaucrats are subject to. The novel data set contains quantitative information that was collected to measure the actual implementation success and quality of public sector projects in various sectors. The authors were able to obtain assessments of completion rates for over 4700 public sector projects from 2006. The aggregate budget of these projects was US$800 million. The survey was used to collect data on management practices for 63 organisations of the Federal Civil Service in Nigeria, including central ministries and regional development authorities. For each organisation, the survey captured two dimensions of management discussed earlier: (1) the autonomy provided to bureaucrats and (2) the provision of incentives and monitoring of bureaucrats. The survey also captured employment history, intrinsic motivation and perceptions of organisational corruption of 4100 civil servants of the 63 organisations. The results show that, though management practices correlate with bureaucratic output, the two dimensions of management practice related to autonomy and incentives/monitoring have opposing correlations with public services delivered. An increase in the autonomy of bureaucrats corresponds to a significantly higher project completion rate while an increase in practices related to incentives/monitoring corresponds to significantly lower project completion rates. The negative correlation between the management practices related to incentive/monitoring and project completion rates is more negative for more complex projects and project types that are of greater ambiguity/uncertainty in design. In addition, the results suggest that corruption has a direct and large negative correlation with project completion rates. The findings are consistent with the notion that public agencies are likely to delegate some decision-making to bureaucrats (Simon, 1983). It also provides support for evidence that management practices related to incentives/monitoring have detrimental impacts in a bureaucratic setting.

# Ghana

A similar study was done by Rasul et al. (2021) for Ghana's Civil Service. It examines the relationship between management practices, organisational performance and task clarity for civil servants across 45 public service organisations in Ghana.

The authors collected novel administrative data on 3620 tasks covering a wide range of bureaucratic activities, from procurement and infrastructure to policy development, advocacy, human resource management, budgeting and regulation. They used this data to measure task completion and clarity. The authors also measured management practices through in-person surveys with nearly 3000 professional-grade civil servants in Ghana's central government. This survey was used to construct indices related to the use of incentives and monitoring, autonomy and discretion. The results show that an increase in autonomy/discretion-related practices is associated with an increase in the likelihood that a project task is fully completed. In contrast, an increase in management practices related to incentives/monitoring-is associated with a decrease in the likelihood that a task is fully completed. The findings provide support for theories that show that monitoring and incentives' systems can back-fire in core civil service policy-making tasks which are intensive in multi-tasking, coordination and instability (Dixit, 2002; Honig, 2018).

# Uganda

This section considers the impact of using citizen reporting to improve public services. Specifically, it examines using a field experiment to improve solid waste services in Uganda (Buntaine et al., 2021). The authors implemented a large-scale field experiment involving 50 citizen reporters in each of 100 neighbourhoods across Kampala, Uganda, to provide weekly reports to the municipal government about the delivery of solid waste services via an SMS messaging platform. This resulted in the generation of 23,856 reports during a nine-month study period.

The theoretical proposition of the study is that citizen reporting, by providing information to governments about deficiencies in public services, will result in an improvement to public services. This is likely to occur when information is high-quality, aligned with uncertainty, addresses search costs for public service failures and if platforms for collecting information is not onerous to operate. In other words, citizen reporting is used to monitor public service performance. The results show that citizen reporting did not improve performance in public service delivery. It highlights three reasons. First, the processing capacity of public agencies can be overwhelmed by the huge data citizens generate. This is further compounded by the quality and consistency of data transmitted in the citizen reports, which requires a greater commitment from the public service agency to transform the data into actionable information. In other words, data quality perception and capacity to deal with data complexity hinder the impact of monitoring on public service performance management. Second, the study highlights the importance of managerial and organisational continuity, as a necessary condition, for the effectiveness of efforts to improve performance management in public service delivery. The discontinuity of the monitoring platform by the new management team within the Ugandan public service shows the importance of managerial support in performance management. Third, the search costs of the monitoring platform can be an incentive or disincentive for public managers to locate the source of service failures and improve performance management.

# Recommendations

Increasing public service performance management is vital for effective regulation, service delivery and overall government efficiency. It is highly dependent on the quality and commitment of public bureaucrats. Better performance management in public service delivery will increase citizens' trust in government. Besides, performance management can have a significant impact on the motivations and attitudes of public servants. It is important to highlight that public service performance management cannot rely solely on extrinsic incentives, such as annual appraisal exercise of individual performance, to increase productivity. Performance management must be viewed as a continuous cycle that involves defining, planning, monitoring, measuring, evaluating and rewarding or sanctioning individual and team level performance. Hence, for public service delivery to improve, the following seven success factors (Schnell et al.) are important for performance management: (1) performance management should start from the top; (2) organisational and individual goals should be aligned; (3) performance assessment should be tailored to institutional and job characteristics and levels of performance should be adequately differentiated; (4) the judgement of public service manager should be improved and the source of information for performance appraisals should be diversified to ensure objectivity and fairness in assessment; (5) staff should be motivated through intrinsic and extrinsic incentives; (6) staff should be provided adequate opportunities for growth and development; and (7) performance management should be embedded in the organisational culture and practice.

# Conclusion

This chapter examines the importance of public service performance management and appraisal for public service delivery in Sub-Saharan Africa. It studies the impact of two dimensions of management practice in public service delivery: autonomy provided to bureaucrats, provision of incentives and monitoring of bureaucrats. The autonomy dimension captures the degree to which bureaucrats contribute to policy formulation and implementation processes; bureaucrats can easily be reorganised to respond to best practices and project peculiarities. This dimension encompasses several theoretical views in the public administration literature. From the view that bureaucrats should be assigned decision-making roles and given the freedom to rely on their professionalism to deliver public services, to the perspective that the divergence between society and bureaucracy objectives necessitates a rule-based system of public administration to ensure acceptable and consistent levels of public service delivery. The incentives/monitoring management dimension capture the extent to which indicators of project performance are gathered, reviewed and used to reward bureaucrats. Theoretically, it posits that performance incentives and monitoring have a positive impact on organisational performance. The results from examining management practices of bureaucrats in African countries such as Nigeria, Ghana and Uganda show that an increase in the autonomy of bureaucrats corresponds to an increase in the completion rate of public projects whereas an increase in incentives and monitoring reduces the rate of public project completion. The negative impact of incentives on completion rates might be because certain features of the public sector make uncertain the impact of incentives such as multiple principals (the action of one government bureaucracy or service agency produce externalities), multiple tasks (most public agencies perform several tasks and sometimes do not have a clear objective), lack of competition (most government agencies are monopolies), motivating agents (intrinsic motivation of public service agents may be crowded out by performance incentives). One of the suggested solutions to this is the promotion of management practices through activating public servants' public service motivation (PSM) to channel their service delivery for the good of the public and society. This motivation may help public managers to engage in ethical decisions and behaviour. PSM comprises four components: self-sacrifice, commitment to public values, attraction to public service, and compassion. Each component affects ethical behaviour through ethical intent which promotes the willingness of public servants to report ethical problems to management. This will benefit public service performance management (Bellé, 2012, 2014) and also the integrity of public sectors.

# References

Bellé, N. (2012). Experimental evidence on the relationship between public service motivation and job performance. *Public Administration Review, 73*(1), 143–153. https://doi.org/10.1111/j.1540-6210.2012.02621.x

Bellé, N. (2014). Leading to make a difference: A field experiment on the performance effects of transformational leadership, perceived social impact, and public service motivation. *Journal of Public Administration Research and Theory, 24*(1), 109–136. https://doi.org/10.1093/jopart/mut033

Bellé, N. (2015). Performance-related pay and the crowding out of motivation in the public sector: A randomized field experiment. *Public Administration Review, 75*(2), 230–241. https://doi.org/10.1111/puar.12313

Brewer, G. A., & Selden, S. C. (1998). Whistle blowers in the Federal Civil Service: New evidence of the public service ethic. *Journal of Public Administration Research and Theory, 8*(3), 413–440. https://doi.org/10.1093/oxfordjournals.jpart.a024390

Buntaine, M. T., Hunnicutt, P., & Komakech, P. (2021). The challenges of using citizen reporting to improve public services: A field experiment on solid waste Services in Uganda. *Journal of Public Administration Research and Theory, 31*(1), 108–127. https://doi.org/10.1093/jopart/muaa026

Colella, A., Paetzold, R. L., Zardkoohi, A., & Wesson, M. J. (2007). Exposing pay secrecy. *Academy of Management Review, 32*(1), 55–71. https://doi.org/10.5465/amr.2007.23463701

Dahlstrom, C., & Lapuente, V. (2010). Explaining cross-country differences in performance-related pay in the public sector. *Journal of Public Administration Research and Theory, 20*(3), 577–600. https://doi.org/10.1093/jopart/mup021

DeSteno, D. (2015). Compassion and altruism: How our minds determine who is worthy of help. *Current Opinion in Behavioral Sciences, 3*, 80–83. https://doi.org/10.1016/j.cobeha.2015.02.002

Dixit, A. (2002). Incentives and organizations in the public sector: An interpretative review. *The Journal of Human Resources, 37*(4), 696. https://doi.org/10.2307/3069614

Dunleavy, P. (1994). The globalization of public services production: Can government be 'Best in World'? *Public Policy and Administration, 9*(2), 36–64. https://doi.org/10.1177/095207679400900204

Dunleavy, P., Margetts, H., Bastow, S., & Tinkler, J. (2005). New public management is dead—long live digital-era governance. *Journal of Public Administration Research and Theory, 16*(3), 467–494. https://doi.org/10.1093/jopart/mui057

Finer, H. (1941). Administrative responsibility in democratic government. *Public Administration Review, 1*(4), 335. https://doi.org/10.2307/972907

Fishenden, J., & Thompson, M. (2013). Digital government, open architecture, and innovation: Why public sector IT will never be the same again. *Journal of Public Administration Research and Theory, 23*(4), 977–1004. https://doi.org/10.1093/jopart/mus022

Friedrich, C. (1978). Public policy and the nature of administrative responsibility. In F. Rourke (Ed.), *Bureaucratic power in National Politics* (3rd ed., pp. 165–175). Little Brown.

Gans-Morse, J., Kalgin, A., Klimenko, A., Vorobyev, D., & Yakovlev, A. (2021). Public service motivation as a predictor of corruption, dishonesty, and altruism. *Journal of Public Administration Research and Theory*. Advance online publication. https://doi.org/10.1093/jopart/muab018

Hasnain, Z., Manning, N., & Pierskalla, H (2012). *Performance-related Pay in the Public Sector: A Review of Theory and Evidence*. World Bank Policy Research Working Paper 6043. https://documents.worldbank.org/en/publication/documents-reports/documentdetail/666871468176639302/performance-related-pay-in-the-public-sector-a-review-of-theory-and-evidence

Honig, D. (2018). *Navigation by judgment: Why and when top-down management of foreign aid doesn't work / Dan Honig*. Oxford University Press.

Ingraham, P. W. (2007). *In pursuit of performance: Management systems in state and local government. Johns Hopkins studies in governance and public management*. Johns Hopkins University Press.

Kwon, I. (2014). Motivation, discretion, and corruption. *Journal of Public Administration Research and Theory, 24*(3), 765–794. https://doi.org/10.1093/jopart/mus062

Lynn, L. E., Heinrich, C. J., & Hill, C. J. (2000). Studying governance and public management: Challenges and prospects. *Journal of Public Administration Research and Theory, 10*(2), 233–262. https://doi.org/10.1093/oxfordjournals.jpart.a024269

Margetts, H., & Dunleavy, P. (2013). The second wave of digital-era governance: A quasi-paradigm for government on the web. *Philosophical Transactions. Series A, Mathematical, Physical, and Engineering Sciences, 371*(1987), 20120382. https://doi.org/10.1098/rsta.2012.0382

Marsden, D., & Richardson, R. (1994). Performing for pay? The effects of 'merit pay' on motivation in a public service. *British Journal of Industrial Relations, 32*(2), 243–261. https://doi.org/10.1111/j.1467-8543.1994.tb01043.x

Meyer-Sahling, J.-H., Mikkelsen, K. S., & Schuster, C. (2019). The causal effect of public service motivation on ethical behavior in the public sector: Evidence from a large-scale survey experiment. *Journal of Public Administration Research and Theory, 29*(3), 445–459. https://doi.org/10.1093/jopart/muy071

Miller, G. J., & Whitford, A. B. (2006). The Principal's moral Hazard: Constraints on the use of incentives in hierarchy. *Journal of Public Administration Research and Theory, 17*(2), 213–233. https://doi.org/10.1093/jopart/mul004

Miller, G. J., & Whitford, A. B. (2016). *Above politics.* Cambridge University Press. https://doi.org/10.1017/CBO9781139017688

Moynihan, D. P., Fernandez, S., Kim, S., LeRoux, K. M., Piotrowski, S. J., Wright, B. E., & Yang, K. (2011). Performance regimes amidst governance complexity. *Journal of Public Administration Research and Theory, 21*(Supplement 1), i141–i155. https://doi.org/10.1093/jopart/muq059

Olken, B. A., & Pande, R. (2012). Corruption in developing countries. *Annual Review of Economics, 4*(1), 479–509. https://doi.org/10.1146/annurev-economics-080511-110917

Pollitt, C., & Bouckaert, G. (2011). *Public management reform: A comparative analysis: New public management, governance, and the neo-Weberian state / Christopher Pollitt and Geert Bouckaert* (3rd ed.). Oxford University Press.

Rasul, I., & Rogger, D. (2018). Management of Bureaucrats and Public Service Delivery: Evidence from the Nigerian civil service. *The Economic Journal, 128*(608), 413–446. https://doi.org/10.1111/ecoj.12418

Rasul, I., Rogger, D., & Williams, M. J. (2021). Management, organizational performance, and task clarity: Evidence from Ghana's civil service. *Journal of Public Administration Research and Theory, 31*(2), 259–277. https://doi.org/10.1093/jopart/muaa034

Schnell, S., Mihes, D., Sobjak, A., & van Acker, W. *Performance Management in the Public Administration.* World Bank. Website. https://openknowledge.worldbank.org/handle/10986/35921

Simon, W. H. (1983). Legality, bureaucracy, and class in the welfare system. *The Yale Law Journal, 92*(7), 1198. https://doi.org/10.2307/796270

Stazyk, E. C., & Davis, R. S. (2015). TAKING THE 'HIGH ROAD': DOES PUBLIC SERVICE MOTIVATION ALTER ETHICAL DECISION MAKING PROCESSES? *Public Administration, 93*(3), 627–645. https://doi.org/10.1111/padm.12158

Thomann, E., van Engen, N., & Tummers, L. (2018). The necessity of discretion: A Behavioral evaluation of bottom-up implementation theory. *Journal of Public Administration Research and Theory, 28*(4), 583–601. https://doi.org/10.1093/jopart/muy024

Weibel, A., Rost, K., & Osterloh, M. (2010). Pay for performance in the public sector—benefits and (hidden) costs. *Journal of Public Administration Research and Theory, 20*(2), 387–412. https://doi.org/10.1093/jopart/mup009

Wright, B. E., Hassan, S., & Park, J. (2016). Does a public service ethic encourage ethical behaviour? Public service motivation, ethical leadership and the willingness to report ethical problems. *Public Administration, 94*(3), 647–663. https://doi.org/10.1111/padm.12248

# 9

# Leveraging Public Service Performance Management to Enhance Public Service Delivery: A Contemporary Perspective

Desmond Tutu Ayentimi

## Introduction

The idea of a public sector organisation or a public service agency/institution comes in countless forms and shapes. For example, the most noticeable public service organisations are schools, the police service and hospitals, although there are several less obvious public service organisations including regulatory agencies, public transport service providers and state-owned enterprises. The goal to meet public interests by public service organisations varies significantly from the profit maximisation aim of private sector organisations. Generally, performance management in public service organisations may sometimes be more complex because of the difficulties in measuring the output of public services. There can also be occasions where there is not enough relationship between the costs of delivering the service and the amount of resources utilised

D. T. Ayentimi (✉)
University of Tasmania, Hobart, TAS, Australia
e-mail: desmond.ayentimi@utas.edu.au

© The Author(s), under exclusive license to Springer Nature Switzerland AG 2022    **171**
K. Ogunyemi et al. (eds.), *Ethics and Accountable Governance in Africa's Public Sector,*
*Volume I*, Palgrave Studies of Public Sector Management in Africa,
https://doi.org/10.1007/978-3-030-95394-2_9

(Hvidman & Andersen, 2013). For example, considering the case of a subsidised public transport service, the cost of running the public bus system is expected to be fixed, yet it is not contingent on the number of commuters using the service, making it complicated to determine the amount of resources to be used on public transport service.

Over the last two decades, some significant progress has been made in several areas across sub-Saharan Africa, ranging from improved governance systems to economic and political stability, and the fight against extreme poverty and underdevelopment (Ayentimi, 2020a; Engida & Bardill, 2013). Notwithstanding this progress there remain significant socio-economic, technological, political, cultural and structural challenges that need to be addressed for Africa's public service to provide improved service quality to its growing population. In fact, many commentators, civil society organisations and individuals across the region have consistently bemoaned the poor service delivery systems of public service organisations and, in some cases, across private sector organisations that are expected to demonstrate exceptional service delivery owing to their profit maximisation goal (Ayentimi, 2020a). Unquestionably, the poor public service delivery in Africa has been attributed to several factors. These include the declining public service budget allocations, poor human capital as an outcome of the consequential reduction in career opportunities in public service, lack of training and development opportunities, recruitment biases and political interference (Abane & Phinaitrup, 2020; Hartley & Seymour, 2011).

Indeed, alongside several public sector challenges, one important issue that has taken centre stage within contemporary public service in Africa is the widespread public perception of state organisations and/or governments as corrupt, unproductive and wasteful (Ohemeng et al., 2018). It is generally assumed that corruption, mismanagement and poor work culture and ethic are rooted within public service in Africa, opening the door-to-poor public service delivery compared to the private sector, where these issues are not too prevalent, although they do exist. Interestingly, there is no doubt that poor work culture and ethic, political obstruction and corruption in Africa's public service weakened not only the capability of public service to deliver quality service but also the efficiency and professionalism of public service organisations. Not long ago, Abane and Phinaitrup (2020) examined the influence of organisational subculture and national culture on performance management in sub-Saharan Africa and found that both sub-group and general societal norms impacted performance management outcomes. It is important to contend here that by failing to uphold the principles of professionalism, Africa's public service will fail to achieve its objectives as well as meet the needs and aspirations of its growing population. Strategically, addressing issues of public service professionalism—competencies, integrity (ethics), positive mindset (attitude)—in Africa needs to be urgently considered.

The recent emerging technological transformation, also acknowledged as the Fourth Industrial Revolution (4IR), which is a combination of technologies supporting biological, digital and physical innovations, is spreading at an unmatched speed and disrupting virtually every industry, economy (both developed and less developed) and every aspect of human life (Ayentimi, 2020b). Besides the remarkable changes taking place as an outcome of the interconnectedness of sovereign states into a global economy (globalisation), the role of the state or government, and by extension public service, is also evolving. The new and growing global challenges have either increased or altered the expectations from public service organisations, making existing processes and structure of public service management outdated. Indeed, meeting the current needs and future challenges of Africa demands not only the rebuilding of public service structures to deliver value for money, but a public service that is performance based and citizen oriented. While the Africans of today are no longer impressed by the time-consuming processes, the disrespect from service delivery representatives and the unending hierarchical levels of authority, they are increasingly demanding public service professionalism, quality service, timeliness and value for money (Kaupa & Atiku, 2020).

In the phase of the global Covid-19 pandemic, where public sector resources are overstretched, maintaining and improving public service delivery while keeping costs in check must be a priority for most governments in Africa. Leveraging public service performance management to enhance public service delivery remains a global priority as public service organisations across the globe are increasingly under pressure to deliver improved service quality and to ensure value for money. Leveraging public service performance management is a key driver for Africa's future development success, yet in too many public service organisations across the region, performance management and appraisal systems are inundated with operational complexities. This chapter highlights the landscape of public service performance management in Africa, with a focus on the underlying complications undermining their effectiveness and success. The chapter further explores how public service organisations in Africa can leverage performance management to improve the efficiency of public service.

# Performance Management Challenges in Public Service in Africa

Africa consists of 54 countries characterised by diverse economic development paths, political ideology, history, language and culture, making it the most diverse continent in the world. However, whether the discussion of public service performance is centred on empirical studies or on anecdotal evidence, there is a strong resemblance of poor public service across the different sub-regions. From the North of the continent, Errami and Cargnello (2018) argued that public service performance in Morocco is characteristic of most developing societies, in that dysfunctional administrative structures combined with managerial challenges were undermining the successful adoption of New Public Management (NPM) as well as public sector reforms. Bergh (2009) found that accountability in the public service remains constrained in Morocco because of the nature of its governance system. Meanwhile, in Tunisia, Brockmeyer et al. (2015) noted that the promotion system is either automatic or in most cases based on seniority, as performance appraisal is practically absent in the public service. Therefore, there is the absence of appropriate relationship between individual performance, compensation and promotion.

Reflecting on the performance of Africa's public service from the East, Obong'o (2009) argued that poor public sector performance has been a prime concern which is undermining Kenya's attainment of sustainable development. The author highlighted political interference, inflated staff establishment, mismanagement and excessive regulations and controls to be negatively affecting public service performance. In Uganda, Lutwama et al. (2013) identified several loopholes in the implementation of health workers' performance management. These include poor planning, shortcomings in setting performance targets, lack of clearly defined performance standards and indicators, poor rewarding mechanisms and unsatisfactory performance feedback. In Ethiopia, Debela and Hagos (2012) noted that public service performance management is incoherent at the top, which directly undermines public sector accountability.

In the western part of the sub-region, Ohemeng's (2009) study of performance management in Ghana's public service highlights capacity and institutional constraints including institutional fragmentation, leadership, culture and public apathy. The author argues that these constraints make it extremely challenging to achieve the anticipated outcomes of a performance management system. The author further noted that if these constraints are not addressed, the public service performance management system will fail to achieve the desired outcomes in Ghana. Similarly, Owusu (2006) found differences in characteristics between well-performing and poorly performing public service organisations in Ghana. These differences are evident in the recruitment and remuneration practices. The author suggests that transforming poorly performing public service organisations is more complicated and goes beyond just remuneration and hiring practices. It demands underlying changes in the organisation's culture. Meanwhile, in Sierra Leone's public service, Kanneh and Haddud (2016) highlighted several key challenges such as lack of strategic planning, lack of knowledge by staff, lack of leadership commitment, lack of resources, lack of measuring criteria and lack of effective communication.

Drawing evidence from the central part of the sub-region, particularly from the Republic of Congo, Moukouyou-Kouaka and Awolusi (2020) argued that while those expected to evaluate employee performance were not sufficiently trained, senior managers failed to undertake regular employee appraisal as well as encourage career development conversations in the public service. Meanwhile, in the Democratic Republic of Congo, Ragasa et al. (2016) highlighted the lack of funding, the absence of a cohesive and clear policy directive, and the lack of coordination as factors affecting the delivery of public services in rural regions.

Lastly, from Southern Africa, Zinyama et al. (2015) in a review of current performance issues in Zimbabwe noted that the most common complaints were that public service staff were arrogant, lazy, insensitive and uncaring; responded to clients slowly; were unreasonably absent from their workstations; spent work time for private businesses; engaged in lengthy lunch breaks; and practised favouritism in attending to clients. Similarly, in Namibia's public sector, Kaupa and Atiku (2020) highlighted six problems: the existence of silo culture, low level of conformity to process, poor training of implementing officers, lack of consultation, poor communication and lack of flexibility. These challenges have been undermining public service efficiency. In the case of South Africa, Van der Waldt (2006) argued that despite political leaders regularly complaining about the increasing bureaucracy when demonstrating the commitment to improve public services, however, once in office, they generally resist dealing with such issues with the fear of losing political patronage. This is a feature common to most performance improvement programmes in Africa because of fears associated with future elections. Makhubela et al. (2016) found that employees in South Africa's public service perceive their performance appraisals to be unfair and the entire performance management system to be ineffective. Likewise, Cameron (2015) argued that performance management challenges within South Africa's public service can be classified into four categories: the problems of design and measurement, lack of compliance, lack of capacity and accountability.

In recent times across Africa, there has been a welcome move towards thinking about the performance of public service organisations, as evident in the application of NPM and several public sector reforms across the region (Engida & Bardill, 2013). Performance management is a broader concept than performance appraisal; it aims to improve the functional and organisation-wide performance of individuals and teams (Olufemi, 2014). Public service performance management evaluates the improvement being made in relation to the accomplishment of public service goals. It helps to align structures, processes, resources and employees to meet the strategic goals of public service organisations. Yet, in too many public service organisations across the region, performance management and appraisal systems are either too slow or completely broken and submerged in operational difficulties. Africa's public service performance management challenges have countless dimensions ranging from issues of accountability to professionalism, moral rectitude, resources, culture, politics and leadership (Cameron, 2015; Kanneh & Haddud, 2016).

First, a persistent challenge within public service performance management in Africa is the absence of alignment between strategy at the national, regional and district levels; budgeting; and operational planning (Kanneh & Haddud, 2016). This has resulted in the creation of administrative processes in isolation in most public service organisations leading to the absence of alignment between organisational delivery objectives, departmental performance and employee performance within the performance management system.

Second, leadership capability and dedication have a significant influence in supporting and incorporating appropriate administrative structures required to deliver a workable public service performance management system which is critical for public service delivery (Bernecker et al., 2018). Yet, there is a major managerial and leadership challenge in public service organisations driven by several factors such as poor leadership mindset and their lack of appreciation of the fact that performance appraisal in the public service is not a one-off event but needs to be managed and documented periodically through reviews as part of the broader performance management of the organisation.

Third, an entrenched challenge in Africa's public service is that managing public service poor performance is by tradition a reactive action (Engida & Bardill, 2013). In many instances, swift actions to deal with poor performance are not taken, but the effort turns into a regular talk show that is challenging to manage in the long term as the consequences would have been severe. For example, delays in responding to poor performance issues in hospitals and public transport service may result in some loss of lives. Indeed, the reactive nature of managing poor performance is further intensified by the absence of reliable data and valid performance measurements. This happens at various public service organisations across Africa in that performance targets are set but no appropriate measures exist, and in some instances, poor performance measures are developed and implemented without user engagement

(Cameron, 2015). Interestingly, the most worrying situation within public service organisations in Africa is where no data is kept or gathered as proof to track the performance of the organisation and individual employees.

Though private sector organisations operate with limited scrutiny from the public, management depends on a great deal of perks to arouse high productivity and performance in line with their primary concern for maximising profit (Hvidman & Andersen, 2013). But for the public service, where its core concern is the value of societal well-being, the extent to which perks can be used to encourage high performance and productivity is limited. Intrinsic motivation is therefore at the heart of how public service organisations in Africa can inspire the moral desire of their employees to work for the benefit of the public. While we acknowledge that there is not a 'silver bullet approach' to overcoming these challenges in Africa's public service, to some extent, it can be argued that the answers to these challenges are rooted in the capability of aligning public service organisational strategy, budgeting and operational planning with a well-established workable performance management system (Kanneh & Haddud, 2016).

# Leveraging Performance Management to Improve the Efficiency of Public Service in Africa

Across sub-Saharan Africa, there is a welcome move at all administrative levels towards thinking about the performance of public service organisations, as evident in several public sector reforms and the adoption of the NPM (Vyas-Doorgapersad, 2011). In view of this welcoming mindset in public service performance, coupled with the global Covid-19 pandemic where public sector resources are increasingly overstretched, maintaining and improving public service delivery while keeping costs in check must be a priority for most governments. Therefore, leveraging public service performance management to enhance public service delivery remains a priority as public service organisations across the globe and not only in

Africa are under increasing pressure to deliver quality public service. The use of performance goals (targets) in public service organisations in Africa offers an avenue to deliver improved service quality and ensure value for money. As early as the 1980s, several notably Western countries including Australia, Sweden, New Zealand and the UK engaged in public service reforms not only to make public service organisations become more responsive, transparent and accountable, but also to enhance the effectiveness and efficiency of public expenditure while delivering quality public service (Hyndman & McGeough, 2008). These public sector reforms have since been underscored as the NPM in Western countries (Vyas-Doorgapersad, 2011; Ayee, 2005).

One essential characteristic of the NPM concept has been the rising usefulness of performance measures and performance targets to appraise public service organisations. Generally, based on the mission of the organisation, objectives are identified from which specific performance targets are set for each objective. While performance measures are largely through quantifiable output, there is an opportunity to complement that with qualitative performance targets (Hyndman & McGeough, 2008). For example, as the quantitative approach measures the passport issuing authority's performance or productivity using the number of passports issued per period, there is also an opportunity to qualitatively measure the level of client satisfaction with the service, which can be measured using client satisfaction surveys. Within the NPM framework, managers and leaders are expected to provide some explanation of any differences between performance targets and actual performance. Some key strengths of this approach to public service management are that it offers greater guidance to staff and managers and increases accountability of public service organisations (Vyas-Doorgapersad, 2011). A lot of the debate about public service accountability is centred on whether or not staff have acted professionally and morally, meaning that they can account for their use of public resources or have not stolen or mismanaged public funds; but an equally imperative facet of public service accountability, however, is how well public service organisations have performed in terms of efficiency and in meeting the needs and aspirations of the citizens (Cameron, 2015).

A method of making a performance target work is to link it with an incentive scheme (performance-based pay), whereby staff are rewarded for delivering on their performance targets (Bernecker et al., 2018). Incentive schemes are expected to stimulate the interest and desire of staff and managers towards achieving targets. However, establishing a performance-based pay scheme in Africa's public service will be exceptionally challenging if not impossible. This can be attributed to several factors including poor performance measures, the absence of data to track individual performance (Cameron, 2015), biases, favouritism and unfairness in performance appraisals (Makhubela et al., 2016). According to Cameron (2015), performance targets are set but no appropriate measures exist, and in most cases, they are poorly developed in public service organisations in Africa. Benchmarking is commonly advocated as a tool for improving the performance of public service organisations (Braadbaart & Yusnandarshah, 2008). Besides the use of incentive schemes to strengthen performance targets in Africa's public service, benchmarking can offer opportunities to improve public service quality by measuring public service organisations' performance against those exceptional public service organisations. Indeed, Owusu (2006) found differences in characteristics between well-performing and poor public service organisations in Ghana. With such evidence from Ghana, benchmarking can create the space to accelerate improvement opportunities among poorly performing public service organisations as they replicate or mimic patterns of best practices from comparable public service organisations (Bruder Jr. & Gray, 1994). The benefits of public service benchmarking are that it supports both incremental and radical innovation. While the latter supports underlying changes to public service delivery, the former exploits existing processes and structures for improving public service delivery (O'Brien, 2020).

Extending the debate beyond benchmarking is the use of league table metrics to rank public service organisations. While league tables are regularly and widely used within the higher education sector to rank universities, similar techniques can be applied in public service organisations in Africa. The use of league tables as complementary to performance targets not only accelerates competition within public service organisations, but also provides the opportunity to highlight specific areas of the organisation's performance or success (Tillema, 2010) which can be replicated by other organisations. This can provide an incentive to poorly performing public service organisations to improve their ranking in the league table. Despite the benefits of benchmarking and league tables, in Africa, some public service organisations are more highly regarded than others, which is further reflected in the allocation of resources and government support. These differences in recognition (government support) and resource allocation among different public service organisations directly impact on their capacity to compete using the same performance metrics. Second, there are demographic differences and uneven development in areas of Africa where some public service organisations are located. Indeed, those with limited resource allocations and in poorer locations will often likely be performing towards the bottom of such league tables.

# Improving the Efficiency of Public Service in Africa: The Way Forward

Although many commentators, civil society organisations and individuals across the region have consistently bemoaned the poor service delivery system of public service organisations, we have also witnessed some public service organisations and their managers achieve outstanding outcomes on a limited scale and with budget constraints (Owusu, 2006). Primarily, for Africa's public service to perform at its peak level, management and staff in public service will need to define impactful or meaningful performance measures. It will not only offer public service staff and their managers a clear viewpoint of current performance challenges, but also help in crafting future performance objectives. For Bernecker et al. (2018), public service organisations need to realise the best strategic actions to develop systems of measurement for tracking their progress. Developing public service performance targets should be restricted only to targets that can be reliably identified and quantified to help reduce biases and the use of managerial discretion in staff performance appraisals. Given that public service staff will likely obtain personal purpose or intrinsic satisfaction from working for the common good of society, which is an important motivating factor, public service staff should be provided with the opportunity to realise the direct impact of their work on performance.

Second, one of the historic attributes of Africa's public services is that their managers and staff often have a tendency to set non-aspirational performance targets, and in some cases, these are detached from the overarching mission of the organisation. Interestingly, public service organisations in Africa regularly portray the achievement of performance targets yet fall short of national expectations. This can be attributed to the setting of easy performance targets and the desire to receive gratuities linked to meeting annual performance targets. This tendency is very widespread in Africa's public service, typically those responsible for revenue mobilisation, where they regularly meet annual revenue targets, yet (calculated out of 30 countries) average tax-to-GDP rate sits at 16.5% in Africa compared to 34.5% in Organisation for Economic Co-operation and Development (OECD) (Revenue Statistics in Africa, 2020). This is certainly not a justifiable illustration of achieving realistic performance targets when the rate of revenue mobilisation is so low that most governments would have to resort to external borrowings to fund public projects and infrastructure. Therefore, setting stretchy or realistic performance targets in public service organisations in Africa can potentially address the tendency to set non-aspirational targets and further increase staff engagement and inspire staff to think 'outside the box' and innovate to meet public service performance targets (Bernecker et al., 2018).

Third, in a rapidly developing digital revolution, public service organisations in Africa can significantly benefit from several emerging digital tools and technologies to support the sharing of real-time performance management information at all levels and within a broader national or sub-national public service performance framework. In many public service organisations where performance targets even exist, dishonesty, favouritism, managerial discretion and the lack of records often undermine the effectiveness of the performance management system that is expected to facilitate a change in the poor work culture and ethic among public service staff (Ayentimi, 2020a). The use of emerging digital tools and technologies such as digital-enabled platforms can help remedy the lack of records, dishonesty, favouritism and managerial discretion. Digitalisation of work systems increases transparency in monitoring when staff report to work (punctuality) and provides real-time staff attendance and performance data. Tactically, creating digital situation rooms can help address the entrenched problem of worker absenteeism and lateness in Africa's public service as well as the recurring culture of poor records or no records.

In addition, the standard performance appraisal system in Africa's public service tends to be centred on employee's past performance with limited opportunities for fostering a culture of continuous improvement. Managers in public service organisations should engage in motivational or developmental dialogue where performance appraisal discussions focus on constructive feedback and personal development. Building a supportive work culture within public service organisations can ensure the success of motivational or developmental dialogue (Bernecker et al., 2018). Extending the debate on creating a developmental performance appraisal dialogue is the need for public service organisations in Africa to underscore non-financial inducements. Comparatively, the remuneration of public service employees is less competitive compared to their private sector counterparts not only in Africa but across the world. In addition, the growing demographic changes within the labour market further deepen the challenges of public service organisations in attracting adequate talent (Ayentimi, 2020b). For example, as the baby-boomers exit from the job market, public service organisations must forcefully compete with private sector organisations for the few skilled workers. Primarily, while public service organisations in Africa may not be able to compete with private sector organisations on the basis of financial incentives to attract and motivate staff, using positive psychology to reinforce positive non-financial incentives for exceptional performers can further increase employee engagement and motivation (Bernecker et al., 2018). These may include providing staff with work autonomy (freedom to independently work), opportunities for recognition, delegation of responsibilities for staff to lead task forces or special projects and providing flexible work models—remote work or work from home, and flexible work hours. This may offer public service organisations in Africa the opportunity to boost performance, where staff are often intrinsically inspired by their sense of purpose or their contribution to the common good of society.

Furthermore, Africa's public service must invest in building new capability through upskilling and reskilling of existing staff to be able to work differently to deliver improved public service. This reinforces Bernecker et al.'s (2018, p. 9) findings 'that successful government transformations were three times as likely to train initiative leaders in change-leadership skills. They were also twice as likely to offer broader capability-building programs to employees involved in the transformation'. Yet in many public service organisations in Africa, managers and staff often fall short with these important transformative or change-leadership and managerial skills. While it may not be based on empirical evidence, anecdotal evidence within Africa's public service points to the absence of at least three valuable interpersonal skill elements among public service managers: motivating workers, supporting staff career development and giving constructive feedback (Moukouyou-Kouaka & Awolusi, 2020).

Finally, the lack of political will and senior management commitment and support have over the years affected broad-based efforts of Africa's public service to improve performance. Some major failures of Africa's public service are the general lack of stakeholder collaboration across ministries, departments and agencies and other relevant stakeholders as well as the absence of agility to deal with evolving situations. Preferably, there is the need to embrace all aspects of dexterity across Africa's public service delivery. It includes being faster and more adaptive to the viewpoint of citizens or clients (Bernecker et al., 2018). This approach will compel senior management and staff of public service organisations to be intimately involved in developing pertinent initiatives and regularly reviewing progress. Displaying responsive ways of working supports regular interactions and engagement as well as staff empowerment to respond more swiftly to public service initiatives.

## Conclusion

In recent years, there has been some evidence to suggest that legitimate efforts are being made across sub-Saharan Africa to make public service work more useful and cost effective to deliver timely and quality service to the growing population (Abane & Phinaitrup, 2020). Indeed, performance targets and benchmarking within the NPM framework can help to make Africa's public service better. However, fronting up to the technological, governance, economic, social-cultural and leadership challenges demands that Africa's public service adjusts its structures and processes to meet the changing expectations of the population and the evolving role of the state. These adjustments in public service must correspond with the pressures of globalisation not only with the aim to improve public service delivery but also to make sub-Saharan Africa globally competitive (Ayentimi, 2020b).

The economic challenges alone in Africa are of such a scale (magnitude) as they call for new competencies and a formidable political will in public service. Success is contingent on the capability of public service to foresee and plan within a more complex society driven by globalisation. The public service must be prudent in its resource allocation whilst delivering quality and impactful service. At the same time, the technological challenges in Africa are primarily centred on how to exploit the benefits of the internet of things, digitisation and digitalisation (digital transformation), automation, blockchain technology, big data analytics and artificial intelligence, while managing the threats of fast-changing technological environments. In relation to the socio-cultural challenges, Africa's public service must consolidate its capacity to listening to the expectations of its citizens with the view of being responsive, transparent and accountable.

While we acknowledge that sincere efforts are now underway in most parts of Africa, more than ever before, Africa's public service is increasingly under pressure to find ground-breaking solutions to the technological, governance, economic, social-cultural and leadership challenges. Indeed, the present public service in Africa finds itself in the situation of having to do more for its disgruntled citizens with limited resources. This significantly underscores the need to leverage public service performance management to enhance public service delivery.

# References

Abane, J. A., & Phinaitrup, B.-A. (2020). The determinants of performance management outcomes in public organizations in Sub-Saharan Africa: The role of national culture and organizational subcultures. *Public Organization Review, 20*, 511–527.

Ayee, J. R. A. (2005). *Public sector management in Africa*. Economic Research Working Paper Series, African Development Bank.

Ayentimi, D. T. (2020a). Who is a customer? In R. E. Hinson, O. Adeola, T. Lituchy, & A. F. O. Amartey (Eds.), *Customer service management in Africa: A strategic and operational perspective* (pp. 11–22). Routledge.

Ayentimi, D. T. (2020b). The 4IR and the challenges for developing economies. In K. Dayaram, L. Lambey, J. Burgess, & T. W. Afrianty (Eds.), *Developing the workforce in an emerging economy: The case of Indonesia* (pp. 18–30). Routledge.

Bergh, S. I. (2009). Constraints to strengthening public sector accountability through civil society: The case of Morocco. *International Journal of Public Policy, 4*(3–4), 344–365.

Bernecker, A., Klier, J., Stern, S., & Thiel, L. (2018). *Sustaining high performance beyond public-sector pilot projects*. McKinsey & Company. Retrieved April 26, 2020, from https://www.mckinsey.com/industries/public-and-social-sector/our-insights/sustaining-high-performance-beyond-public-sector-pilot-projects

Braadbaart, O., & Yusnandarshah, B. (2008). Public sector benchmarking: A survey of scientific articles, 1990–2005. *International Review of Administrative Sciences, 74*(3), 421–433.

Brockmeyer, A., Khatrouch, M., & Raballand, G. (2015). *Public sector size and performance management: A case-study of post-revolution Tunisia*. Policy Research Working Paper. https://doi.org/10.1596/1813-9450-7159

Bruder, K. A., Jr., & Gray, E. M. (1994). Public sector benchmarking: A practical approach. *Public Management, 76*(9), S9–S14.

Cameron, R. (2015). Performance management in the South African Department of Labour: Smoke and mirrors? *African Journal of Public Affairs, 8*(1), 1–18.

Debela, T., & Hagos, A. (2012). Towards a results-based performance management: Practices and challenges in the Ethiopian public sector. *Journal of Business and Administrative Studies, 4*(1), 79–127.

Engida, T. G., & Bardill, J. (2013). Reforms of the public sector in the light of the new public management: A case of Sub-Saharan Africa. *Journal of Public Administration and Policy Research, 5*(1), 1–7.

Errami, Y., & Cargnello, C. E. (2018). The pertinence of new public management in a developing country: The healthcare system in Morocco. *Canadian Journal of Administrative Sciences, 35*, 304–312.

Hartley, K., & Seymour, L. F. (2011). Towards a framework for the adoption of Business Intelligence in public sector organisations: The case of South Africa. *Proceedings of the South African Institute of Computer Scientists and Information Technologists Conference on Knowledge, Innovation and Leadership in a Diverse, Multidisciplinary Environment*, pp. 116–122.

Hvidman, U., & Andersen, S. C. (2013). Impact of performance management in public and private organizations. *Journal of Public Administration Research and Theory, 24*, 35–58.

Hyndman, N., & McGeough, F. (2008). *NPM and performance measurement: A comparative study of the public sectors in Ireland and the UK.* Irish Accounting Review.

Kanneh, L., & Haddud, A. (2016). Performance management in Sierra Leone public sector organisations. *International Journal of Public Sector Performance Management, 2*(4), 411–429.

Kaupa, S., & Atiku, S. O. (2020). Challenges in the implementation of performance management system in Namibian public sector. *International Journal of Innovation and Economic Development, 6*(2), 25–34.

Lutwama, G. W., Roos, J. H., & Dolamo, B. L. (2013). Assessing the implementation of performance management of health care workers in Uganda. *BMC Health Services Research, 13*, 355. https://doi.org/10.1186/1472 -6963-13-355

Makhubela, M., Botha, P. A., & Swanepoel, S. (2016). Employees' perceptions of the effectiveness and fairness of performance management in a South African public sector institution. *South African Journal of. Human Resource Management, 14*(1), a728. https://doi.org/10.4102/sajhrm.v14i1.728

Moukouyou-Kouaka, G., & Awolusi, O. D. (2020). Factors affecting the performance of public sector practitioners in the Republic of Congo. *Information Management and Business Review, 12*(2), 42–61.

O'Brien, K. (2020). Innovation types and the search for new ideas at the fuzzy front end: Where to look and how often? *Journal of Business Research, 107*, 13–24.

Obong'o, S. O. (2009). Implementation of performance contracting in Kenya. *International Public Management Review, 10*(2), 66–83.

OECD/ATAF/AUC. (2020). *Revenue statistics in Africa 2020.* http://oe.cd/revstatsafrica.     https://www.oecd.org/tax/tax-policy/brochure-revenue-statistics-africa.pdf

Ohemeng, F. L. K. (2009). Constraints in the implementation of performance management systems in developing countries: The Ghanaian case. *International Journal of Cross Cultural Management, 9*(1), 109–132.

Ohemeng, F. L. K., Asiedu, E. A., & Obuobisa-Darko, T. (2018). Giving sense and changing perceptions in the implementation of the performance management system in public sector organisations in developing countries. *International Journal of Public Sector Management, 31*(3), 372–392.

Olufemi, F. J. (2014). Performance management systems and productivity in the public sector: Wither African public administration. *Africa's Public Service Delivery & Performance Review, 2*(3). https://doi.org/10.4102/apsdpr.v2i3.60

Owusu, F. (2006). Differences in the performance of public organisations in Ghana: Implications for public-sector reform policy. *Development Policy Review, 24*(6), 693–705.

Ragasa, C., Ulimwengu, J., Randriamamonjy, J., & Badibanga, T. (2016). Factors affecting performance of agricultural extension: Evidence from Democratic Republic of Congo. *The Journal of Agricultural Education and Extension, 22*(2), 113–143.

Tillema, S. (2010). Public sector benchmarking and performance improvement: What is the link and can it be improved? *Public Money & Management, 30*(1), 69–75.

Van der Waldt, G. (2006). Managing local government performance: Key considerations and challenges. *Journal of Public Administration, 41*(2), 128–143.

Vyas-Doorgapersad, S. (2011). Paradigm shift from New Public Administration to New Public Management: Theory and practice in Africa. *The Journal for Transdisciplinary Research in Southern Africa, 7*(2), 235–250.

Zinyama, T., Nhema, A. G., & Mutandwa, H. (2015). Performance management in Zimbabwe: Review of current issues. *Journal of Human Resources Management and Labor Studies, 3*(2), 1–27.

# 10

# Accountable Governance and Ethical Practice in Africa's Public Sector: Mapping a Path for the Future

Kemi Ogunyemi, Isaiah Adisa, and Robert E. Hinson

## Introduction

The book presents the urgency of the need to improve ethics and accountability standards in government institutions in Africa if the continent is to achieve her developmental goals and improve the quality of life of her

K. Ogunyemi (✉)
Lagos Business School, Pan-Atlantic University, Lagos, Nigeria
e-mail: kogunyemi@lbs.edu.ng

I. Adisa
Olabisi Onabanjo University, Ago-Iwoye, Nigeria

R. E. Hinson
University of Ghana, Accra, Ghana

University of Kigali, Kigali, Rwanda

University of the Free State, Bloemfontein, South Africa
e-mail: rhinson@ug.edu.gh

© The Author(s), under exclusive license to Springer Nature Switzerland AG 2022    **189**
K. Ogunyemi et al. (eds.), *Ethics and Accountable Governance in Africa's Public Sector,*
*Volume I,* Palgrave Studies of Public Sector Management in Africa,
https://doi.org/10.1007/978-3-030-95394-2_10

peoples. Government institutions provide most of the resources and services in Africa and are arguably the largest employers of labour. Tolerating systems that fail to promote and enforce ethical public service behaviours and accountable governance will widen the gap between Africa and other developed regions of the world. In fact, the quest for sustainable development by 2030 is at risk if accountability and ethical practices do not become the norm in our public organisations. It is therefore unsurprising that it is a recurring theme in the preceding chapters that African nations must develop codes of ethical conduct and sound governance policies.

The impact of bad governance is felt in diverse ways: the image of some African nations has become so negative that this has affected the inflow of international tourists and investors. Citizens who could be doing a lot in their countries have moved out of Africa in search of places where there is better governance. The ethical practices and values that the indigenous African nations were known for have been eroded in the guise of westernisation. Competitiveness is low in the business space when contracts are awarded without regard to merit; the costs are passed to direct consumers and to the public—in forms of higher pricing of goods and services, poor quality of public amenities and so on. Recommendations have been presented in this book to map the way forward for the continent for adoption by policy makers, researchers and students. The findings which highlight the causes and implications of bad public governance are also documented.

## Key Governance Gaps Identified

*Ethical problem-solving skills* (Iheanachor and Etim, Chap. 2): Sometimes people are trained to solve problems, but the ethical element is left out of the equation. Thus, they may get used to compartmentalising their actions so that they leave ethics aside when doing their work. This would be a dangerous habit for anyone but much more so for a public servant.

*Conflict of interest education* (Coffie and Hinson, Chap. 3): It is possible that some officials are not well educated regarding conflict of interest. Since occasions of conflict are part of life, there needs to be constant training and retraining on how to handle such dilemmatic situations.

*Public education and behavioural change initiatives* (Coffie and Hinson, Chap. 3): The general public also needs this education as well as some interventions to encourage changes in behaviour.

*Procurement* (Netswera, Chap. 4): Procurement systems are particularly vulnerable. It is disappointing and instructive that, during a pandemic, despite the pathos of the predicament of the people, not all the relief packages were meant to succour people reached their destined recipients. Despite existing elaborate codes of conduct, people could and did misappropriate these packages.

*Access control* (Netswera, Chap. 4): The level of looting of public resources described in this chapter could occur only if there is a situation in which people have sole access to those resources, without adequate checks and balances to monitor what they do with the resources placed in their care.

*Industry lobbying* (Mofuoa, Chap. 5): Wherever there is a high incidence of large corporations or whole industries lobbying regulators or government in general, there are also the dangers of regulatory capture and state capture. In those situations, public servants may no longer be serving the public but might be instead serving their own private interests.

*Fairness in recruitment and other people management processes* (Metz, Chap. 6): Decision-making based on partiality rather than what is best for the organisation needs to be discouraged.

*Anti-corruption initiatives* (Wenyah, Chap. 7): There are several anti-corruption programmes, projects, policies and agencies in the various African countries; however, the results of the exertions have not yet met expectations, perhaps because of the complexity of the problems. The efforts must continue to be multi-dimensional, multi-pronged and multi-agency, as required by the nature and extension of the phenomenon.

*Public service performance management* (Nwokolo, Chap. 8): Performance incentives and monitoring have a positive impact on organisational performance.

*Employee autonomy* (Nwokolo, Chap. 8): An increase in the autonomy of bureaucrats leads to an improvement in the completion rates of public projects. When there are many bottlenecks because people are not empowered to act, then the ensuing 'red tape' can hinder progress in getting things done efficiently.

*Incentive structures* (Nwokolo, Chap. 8): An increase in incentives and monitoring of bureaucrats could, in certain cases, reduce the rate of public project completion. Leaders must be careful not to inadvertently incentivise behaviour that they do not wish to encourage.

*Service performance management* (Ayentimi, Chap. 9): Public service delivery can be enhanced with the right approaches to target-setting and monitoring.

*Restructuring* (Ayentimi, Chap. 9): Structures, processes and procedures can be adjusted to fit the needs of the public consumers of the services as things change, in order to serve them better. Digitisation could make a big difference here.

Table 10.1 presents these findings, showing that there are many governance gaps all over Africa and that ethical leadership still remains a challenge despite government codes and policies in this regard. Hence, some actionable solutions that could work for better governance have been proposed by the chapter contributors to this book.

# Towards Better Governance: Actionable Solutions

Various recommendations have been put forward by the chapter contributors as ways to improve governance and the practice of ethics. What is needed and the way of applying them would naturally differ from country to country, and many more apt solutions are surely not captured here; yet these could serve as springboards for reflection that could lead to other solutions being crafted and adopted. There are ten listed here, and overall, they are smart, realistic and achievable. We have put them together below, also in tabular form (see Table 10.2).

*About handling ethical dilemmas*: It is important to foster zero tolerance for corruption and to establish processes for dealing with offers of or requests for questionable payments. To reduce the incidence of foreseeable conflict of interest situations, it would be helpful to establish a clear stand on avoiding and reporting nepotism and increase levels of transparency in all processes.

**Table 10.1** Accountable governance and ethical practice—governance gaps

| Chapter no. | Authors | Chapter title | Gaps found |
|---|---|---|---|
| Chapter 2 | Nkem Iheanachor and Emmanuel Etim | Ethical Dilemmas and Changing Reality in African Public Sector | • Various factors that have impacted the African public sector, such as Covid-19, PESTEL, the pluralisation cost of service provision, and wicked problems are identified. |
| Chapter 3 | Isaac Sewornu Coffie and Robert E. Hinson | Conflict of Interest in Public Sector Organisations in Africa: Reflections on the Ghanaian, South-African and Kenyan Situation | • Despite the present and past governments to identify and address conflict of interest situations in public sector organisations, conflict of interest remains one of the major sources of corruption in the public sector.<br>• Little attention has been given to public education and behavioural change initiatives as alternative approaches to dealing with conflict-of-interest situations |
| Chapter 4 | Fulufhelo Netswera | The Subversion of the South African Public Accountability Ethics Codes of Conduct in the Name of Disaster Management During COVID-19 Pandemic | • Relief and services procurements are also vulnerable areas to corrupt public officials.<br>• Massive looting of public resources happened, despite clear guidelines for ethical conduct such as the Code of Ethics for parliamentarians and the Code for Good Conduct for public servants and the National Treasury directive for procurement, during the COVID-19 lockdown. |
| Chapter 5 | Khali Mofuoa | 'Thuma Mina' as a New Ethic of Public Service Accountability in South Africa | • State capture in South Africa had eroded public service probity |

(continued)

**Table 10.1** (continued)

| Chapter no. | Authors | Chapter title | Gaps found |
|---|---|---|---|
| Chapter 6 | Thaddeus Metz | African Ethics and Public Governance: Nepotism, Preferential Hiring, and Other Partiality | • Officials are not meant to give out contract to relatives or on the basis family ties, ethnicities or religion.<br>• Yet, ethics does not require state officials to award resources on an utterly impartial basis; they may favour individuals with certain *relationships with the state*, specifically, veterans and victims of state injustice, even when it would cost the public something. |
| Chapter 7 | Samuel Wenyah | Anti-corruption Initiatives in Africa's Public Sector | • There are several agencies and policies combating corruption in the country of analysis; however, less than the ideal has been achieved because of the enormous, pervasive and systemic nature of corruption, which requires a multi-dimensional, multi-pronged and multi-agency response. |
| Chapter 8 | Arinze Nwokolo | Public Service Performance Management | • Performance incentives and monitoring have a positive impact on organisational performance.<br>• An increase in the autonomy of bureaucrats leads to an increase in the completion rate of public projects, while an increase in incentives and monitoring of bureaucrats reduces the rate of public project completion. |
| Chapter 9 | Desmond Tutu Ayentimi | Leveraging Public Service Performance Management to Enhance Public Service Delivery: A Contemporary Perspective | • Performance targets and benchmarking within the NPM framework can help to make Africa's public service better.<br>• Africa's public service must adjust its structures and processes to meet the changing expectations of the population and the evolving role of the state. |

**Table 10.2**  Mapping a path for accountability and ethical practice in Africa

| Chapter | Authors | Title | Recommendations from authors |
|---|---|---|---|
| Chapter 2 | Nkem Iheanachor and Emmanuel Etim | Ethical Dilemmas and Changing Reality in African Public Sector | • Since corrupting public officials may sometimes take the form of a subtle approach originating from the public to make the officer gradually become loyal to one individual or one faction rather than to the whole community, it is important, therefore, to help public officers to avoid falling prey to unexplained and unjustified 'generous' gestures from members of the public who then later require any form of service.<br>• Public officers should avoid the temptation of appointing relatives to work in the same office as them.<br>• Public officers need to exercise a high level of patience and tolerance, especially when they encounter aggressive clients, abusive co-workers and clients with pitiable situations. The core principles and values of the organisation must be defended in all situations. |
| Chapter 3 | Robert E. Hinson and Isaac Sewornu Coffie | Conflict of Interest in Public Sector Organisations in Africa: Reflections on the Ghanaian, South-African and Kenyan Situation | • Behavioural change approaches that use marketing principles and techniques (social marketing) to design effective interventions that seek to elicit voluntary positive changes in attitude towards the handling of conflict-of-interest situations.<br>• It is important to maintain the integrity of official policy and administrative decisions and public management generally, recognising that an unresolved conflict of interest may result in abuse of public office. |

(continued)

**Table 10.2** (continued)

| Chapter | Authors | Title | Recommendations from authors |
|---------|---------|-------|------------------------------|
| Chapter 4 | Fulufhelo Netswera | The Subversion of the South African Public Accountability Ethics Codes of Conduct in the Name of Disaster Management During COVID-19 Pandemic | • COVID-19 investigations should be carried out; suspension and trial of public officials and recouping of corruption funds will signal a turn of a new leaf in the fight against corruption, which should be the new order.<br>• The enforcement of the Code of Ethics and Code of Good Conduct needs to be improved. |
| Chapter 5 | Khali Mofuoa | 'Thuma Mina' as a New Ethic of Public Service Accountability in South Africa | • Thuma Mina is the new ethic of accountability and responsibility for the South African public service to bring about much-needed ethical and accountable governance in South Africa after 'state capture', which eroded public service probity.<br>• The ideology of Thuma Mina should be used to slow the wheels of corruption in South Africa and help government to improve its handling of anti-corruption fight effectively. |
| Chapter 6 | Thaddeus Metz | African Ethics and Public Governance: Nepotism, Preferential Hiring, and Other Partiality | • Honouring people's social nature requires displaying gratitude, expressing remorse and trying to reconcile with those the state has been wronged, all of which the state could achieve by preferential hiring and without promoting substantial discord in society as a result. This does not mean putting personal interest above the collective interest or abusing one's office.<br>• There is a difference between African moral values and Western moral values; this distinction must be understood for proper application. |

(continued)

**Table 10.2**   (continued)

| Chapter | Authors | Title | Recommendations from authors |
|---|---|---|---|
| Chapter 7 | Samuel Wenyah | Anti-corruption Initiatives in Africa's Public Sector | • Political parties should be made to disclose the source of funding for their political activities.<br>• Countries should put in more effort in enforcing existing anti-corruption laws. Clear targets should be set, and there should be a clear pathway to achieving the set objectives.<br>• States must also establish measures to properly investigate, prosecute and legally sanction all reported cases of corruption, with no exception.<br>• Training and education of public administrators in ethics and ethical behaviour is important. |
| Chapter 8 | Arinze Nwokolo | Public Service Performance Management | • Bureaucrats should be assigned decision-making roles and given the freedom to rely on their professionalism to deliver public services, while appreciating the perspective that the divergence between society and bureaucracy objectives also necessitates a rule-based system of public administration to ensure acceptable and consistent levels of public service delivery.<br>• The promotion of management practices through activating public servants' public service motivation (PSM) can be used to channel their service delivery for the good of the public and society. |
| Chapter 9 | Desmond Tutu Ayentimi | Leveraging Public Service Performance Management to Enhance Public Service Delivery: A Contemporary Perspective | • For Africa's public service to perform at its peak level, management and staff in public service will need to define impactful or meaningful performance measures.<br>• Africa's public service must invest in building new capability through upskilling and reskilling of existing staff to be able to work differently to deliver improved public service. |

*About achieving change:* Adopt behavioural change approaches—using marketing principles and techniques (e.g. social marketing) to design and implement effective interventions that seek to elicit voluntary change in people's attitude towards conflict of interest. Involving young people in design and implementation could also help to drive relevance and acceptance.

*About establishing procurement security:* Maintain the integrity of official policy and administrative decisions and public management generally, recognising that an unresolved conflict of interest may result in abuse of public office. Codes of ethical conduct should include stricter provisions about giving and receiving gifts for those involved in the procurement processes. Checks and balances for the procurement function should also be well established.

*About dealing with wrongdoing firmly:* After carrying out investigations, enforce the provisions of the codes—suspension and trial of public officials and recouping of corruption funds. Impartiality in applying sanctions is important for passing across the right message. Whistleblowing systems that are safe for the whistleblower should also be put in place so that people who genuinely see things going wrong can report this.

*About building a strong value system and grooming ethical leaders:* Adopt 'Thuma Mina' as an ethic of stewardship and public service accountability. Thuma Mina is the new ethic of accountability and responsibility for the South African public service to bring about much-needed ethical and accountable governance in South Africa after the state capture which had eroded public service probity. Other African countries can find similar indigenous values in their own cultures or adopt Thuma Mina as well.

*About recruiting and managing people:* There must be a very strong reason for bringing in a relative to the workplace or awarding a contract to a relative. Preferential hiring (and contracting) can be done in some circumstances but only when it is for the good of the organisation and not for personal advantage. If it is done, special attention must be paid to performance management so that the new conflicts of interest about monitoring the quality of service delivery do not arise or are appropriately handled.

*About carrying out anti-corruption initiatives:* Those given this responsibility must be unrelenting and impartial in their efforts to enforce existing anti-corruption laws. This could proactively include repeated in-depth anti-corruption training and encourage anti-corruption risk assessment exercises carried out with staff buy-in, and reactively ensure clear and concrete processes for dealing with and sanctioning those proven to be involved in corruption cases.

*About managing public service performance*: Setting concrete and realistic objectives as well as clear performance measures and timelines would constitute a guide to staff as to what progress they are making regarding the standards of service delivery they are meant to achieve. It would also incorporate feedback opportunities which could then spur continuous improvement.

*About granting autonomy to staff within limits*: Increased autonomy would mean that the individuals are given the freedom, albeit with boundaries, to do some decision-making in their organisational roles. This could reduce the time to deliver service and raise levels of confidence and trust in individual public officials and in the system as well. It could also affect the ease-of-doing-business indices for each country and boost their economy.

*About building capacity*: Training and upskilling and reskilling people would improve expertise and preparedness to deliver the right quality of service to the public. In addition, technology can be harnessed to raise the systemic capacity to deliver service. Again, staff would require training on the optimal use of such technology.

# Conclusion

Unethical practices and avoidance of accountability occur everywhere; however, they seem to be more noticeable in Africa, perhaps because the forms they take are less sophisticated. Whatever the case, the desired change in public sector ethos and public service delivery in Africa must start with individuals. Individuals need to cultivate and/or maintain as well as demand a culture of integrity, sacrifice and accountability. Also, African governments must create systems that do promote ethical practices by implementing policies that encourage good behaviour and punish erring public officials. Ethical codes of conduct need to be better implemented and institutionalised for every government institution, and the leaders of those institutions must lead the way in abiding by the code. These steps will help revive public trust and can also elicit corresponding good behaviour from the private sector.

# Index

K. Ogunyemi et al. (eds.), *Ethics and Accountable Governance in Africa's Public Sector,*
*Volume I,* Palgrave Studies of Public Sector Management in Africa,
https://doi.org/10.1007/978-3-030-95394-2_1

9 783030 953935